A PRESIDENTIAL NATION

A PRESIDENTIAL NATION

Causes, Consequences, and Cures

MICHAEL A. GENOVESE

Loyola Chair of Leadership
Loyola Marymount University

WESTVIEW PRESS

A Member of Perseus Books Group

Westview Press was founded in 1975 in Boulder, Colorado, by notable publisher and intellectual Fred Praeger. Westview Press continues to publish scholarly titles and high-quality undergraduate- and graduate-level textbooks in core social science disciplines. With books developed, written, and edited with the needs of serious nonfiction readers, professors, and students in mind, Westview Press honors its long history of publishing books that matter.

Published by Westview Press,
A Member of the Perseus Books Group

Find us on the World Wide Web at www.westviewpress.com.

Every effort has been made to secure required permissions for all text, images, maps, and other art reprinted in this volume.

Westview Press books are available at special discounts for bulk purchases in the United States by corporations, institutions, and other organizations. For more information, please contact the Special Markets Department at the Perseus Books Group, 2300 Chestnut Street, Suite 200, Philadelphia, PA 19103, or call (800) 810-4145, ext. 5000, or e-mail special.markets@perseusbooks.com.

Library of Congress Cataloging-in-Publication Data
Genovese, Michael A.
    A presidential nation : causes, consequences, and cures / Michael A. Genovese.
        p. cm.
    Includes bibliographical references and index.
    ISBN 978-0-8133-4721-9 (pbk. : alk. paper) —
ISBN 978-0-8133-4722-6 (e-book)
    1. Presidents—United States—History.   2. Executive power—United States—History.   3. United States—Politics and government.   I. Title.
    JK516.G467 2013
    352.230973—dc23

                                                           2012002584

10 9 8 7 6 5 4 3 2 1

To Pookey

CONTENTS

Contents

LIST OF ILLUSTRATIONS

Preface

Taking a leisurely stroll through the nation's capital, one is struck by the sheer power and force of the architecture. Large, imposing buildings line the streets; the city oozes power. Sprinkled here and there are the Washington Monument, the Jefferson Memorial, the Lincoln Memorial, the FDR Memorial . . . grand tributes to our presidential icons.

Why do we devote monuments to the presidents? Why do we honor the presidents so? Why don't we do the same for Congress (the people's branch) or the Courts (the great defenders of our rights and liberties)? Why not "the people"? What makes the presidency so special?

And in so honoring presidents at the expense of others, what message are we sending? Does the public, exposed as it is to the homages to the presidency, begin to view the president as a genuine Superman, powerful and good? Does this image accurately reflect the political world that presidents occupy? Do we "think" the president is more powerful than he or she truly is? By ignoring the separation of powers and the roadblocks faced by the presidents, do we give a false impression of both the power of the office and the systemic realities of the separation of powers? Are we doing constitutional violence when we elevate the presidency to such exalted heights while virtually ignoring Congress and the courts? Ours is, after all, a government of three branches, not one, and in focusing so much attention and adulation on but one office, we demean the others and undermine the constitutional order of separation of powers and checks and balances.

How, we might justifiably ask, can a mere court or Congress stand in the way of our mighty president? Who are they to bring down this most magnificent office? This, of course, sets up a false image and a false idol. The president *is not*, at least constitutionally, the government, and the office is not all-powerful or imperial. The president shares powers with Congress, and each branch has a role in checking the others.

This book is a brief study of how the presidency—an office limited by the Constitution and separation of powers—became the centerpiece of American government. It is about how we became a presidential nation.

I wish to thank but a few of the many people who helped bring this book to print. At Loyola Marymount University, Brian Whitaker, administrative assistant at the Institute for Leadership Studies, and researchers Becky Hartley, Matt Candau, Katie McGrath, and Brianna Bruns were all invaluable. Toby Wahl at Westview Press was a kind and understanding editor. And Gaby, my wife, I thank you for so very many things, especially for giving me so much guilt-free writing time.

1

On Becoming a Presidential Nation

Still the question recurs "can we do it better?" The dogmas of the quiet past are inadequate to the stormy present. The occasion is piled high with difficulty, and we must rise with the occasion. As our case is new, so we must think anew, and act anew.

—Abraham Lincoln, annual message to
Congress, December 1, 1862

For better or worse, the United States is today a presidential nation. It wasn't supposed to be that way. When created 235 years ago, this experiment in self-government explicitly rejected the trappings of monarchy and the centralization of power that characterized executive tyranny. Ours would be a new way of thinking, a new way of being, a new method of governing.

The brave men and women who declared their independence from Great Britain did so in hopes of forging a new form of government, one built upon the foundation laid out in the Declaration of Independence. It was a bold and risky venture. Not only would they take on the world's mightiest military power, but they also had designs on establishing a new form of government. This truly was the greatest generation. In inventing the presidency, the framers sought to distance themselves from the perceived tyranny of the British past, as they jettisoned the ways of monarchy to embrace a more republican, constitutional, and limited executive. Such a model of executive power had never been tried before. Many believed it to be unworkable and doomed to failure.

What I will argue in this book is that in rebelling against the British, the framers rejected the British model of executive power, saw executive tyranny as the chief danger to be avoided, and thus invented a circumscribed presidency under a constitutional republic, with the rule of law and a system of separation of powers and checks and balances. In this system, Congress had more significant constitutional powers than the presidency yet was designed to move slowly. On the other hand, the presidency was a more adaptable and streamlined office, able to move quickly. Over time presidential power has risen and congressional power declined, to the point where today, the United States has become a presidential nation with a near-imperial presidency that, while not coming literally full circle from the monarchical government against which it rebelled in 1776, nonetheless has more in common with the imperial powers of a king than the constitutional power of the presidency of 1787.

Twenty years ago, to have written the above would have been noncontroversial and not in dispute. Today, the purposes and origins of the presidency are a battlefield. What has changed to cause this dramatic shift? What shattered the old consensus and caused the new rift in thinking? Simply put, 9/11.

It has often been said that "9/11 changed everything." Of the changes sparked by the attacks of September 11, 2001, one that many feel has come back to haunt the United States is the willing suspension of the rule of law and the system of checks and balances that so aptly characterized and so ably served the system of separation of powers of the US government for more than two hundred years. In the aftermath of 9/11, as in the wake of other crises and emergencies in the past, the United States ratcheted up presidential power and spiraled down the role and authority of Congress. Crisis again trumped the rule of law, creating what presidential scholar Clinton Rossiter more than sixty years ago dubbed "the constitutional dictatorship" and what in the 1970s historian Arthur M. Schlesinger Jr. called "the imperial presidency."

The United States invested power and responsibility in the hands of one man, the president, and trusted him to protect us, punish our enemies, and make us feel safe again. For a brief time, it seemed trust well placed. President George W. Bush prosecuted a short and seemingly victorious war against the Taliban government in Afghanistan, a government that had been harboring terrorist leader Osama bin Laden and his al-Qaeda terrorist network. The Department of Homeland Security was established to protect us at home. Congress played the willing role of enabler, rubber-stamping virtually all requests from the administration or, more often, turning a blind eye to unilateral actions taken by the president, even as those actions trampled on the powers of Congress itself. And when a few citizens raised objections, the president sent his attorney general, John Ashcroft, to Congress to suggest that not supporting the president amounted to "aiding and abetting the enemy," the textbook definition of treason. It worked, silencing the few critics brave enough to raise questions about the administration's actions . . . at least for a time.

While President Bush's popularity hovered in the 80 percent range, the opposition meekly cowered like lambs. It was presidential government, and Congress and the courts proved little more than minor annoyances to the presidential leviathan. However, two things happened to destroy the period of presidential dominance: the war in Iraq and Hurricane Katrina.

In March 2003, the president launched a war of choice against Saddam Hussein in Iraq on the flimsiest of evidence, suggesting that

Saddam had "weapons of mass destruction" (he did not), would use them against the United States (he was in no position to), was sponsoring terrorists (again, only marginal evidence has surfaced to support the claim of extensive support for terrorism), had links to al-Qaeda (Osama bin Laden actually opposed Saddam, who was not, in al-Qaeda's eyes, a true Muslim), and was linked to the 9/11 attacks against the United States (again, no). As each rationale eventually crumbled under the weight of the evidence, the president switched to a new and more visionary rationale: to bring democracy to the Middle East! Instead, civil and sectarian war erupted, and the United States was stuck in the middle.

The other event that led to the downfall of the president's privileged position was Hurricane Katrina, which struck in and around New Orleans in the fall of 2005. The administration's response to this tragedy was slow and blundering. As Americans watched the tragedy unfold on their television screens, they witnessed government mistake after mistake and death after death. Where was the Federal Emergency Management Agency? Where was the National Guard? Where was the administration's response to this domestic tragedy? Katrina called into question claims by the administration that it was capable, caring, and in control. Americans could see that the opposite was the case. And they blamed the president. Bush's popularity plummeted to the 30 percent range. It was a drop of more than fifty points (the most ever) from the high of 90 percent that the president reached right after 9/11 to the depth of 32 percent in 2007. It would fall to the 20 percent range in 2008.

The decline of George W. Bush's imperial status gives us the opportunity to reexamine the status of presidential power in an age of terrorism. Must the United States be a presidential nation, or are there alternative models to which we might adhere? The consensus of the 1980s and '90s concerning the scope and limits of presidential power has, today, morphed into a battle for the "true" meaning of presidential power. Today, there are essentially four "camps," or views, on the proper scope of presidential power: the presidential supremacists, those believing that necessity requires a powerful president, the constitutionalists, and the presidential leadership camp.

Camp 1: The Presidential Supremacists: One camp argues that the imperial presidency is not new. In fact, you can find it right there in the Constitution. Relying on what has come to be known as the *unitary theory* of presidential power, this view maintains that the executive vesting clause of the Constitution (Article II, Section 1) gives the president all executive power. When this clause is combined with the commander-in-chief clause (Article II, Section 2), the president has a vast array of constitutional powers that make him supreme in the US system. John Yoo, former George W. Bush Office of Legal Counsel lawyer and author of the famous "torture memo," is the leading exponent of this view.[1] Other proponents of the unitary executive view do not always go to the lengths Yoo does, yet still see a powerful presidency whose authority is grounded in the Constitution.[2]

Camp 2: Necessity and Presidential Power: Another camp argues that, indeed, the framers created a circumscribed presidency, bounded by the rule of law and a system of separation of powers that checks and balances the branches. This enchaining of the presidency reflected the framers' great fear of centralized executive power (tyrannophobia), and they thus created a Madisonian system that limited presidential authority. Yet this system is seen as inappropriate for a superpower in an age of terrorism, and so, in their view, we must abandon Madison's limited executive in favor of a president fully armed to govern in the modern era. Necessity demands strong presidential power to meet the threats of a dangerous world. And although the Constitution does not allow it, necessity requires it.[3]

Camp 3: The Constitutionalists: The third camp argues that the framers were intent on inventing a limited presidency under the rule of law. They do not believe we need to abandon the Madisonian system of checks and balances in the modern world. In fact, they see the separation of powers as a great benefit for the United States. The Madisonian system both prevents tyranny and, when properly utilized, produces a sound, consensus-oriented government. This camp believes that our great strength—not our great weakness—is the separation of powers.[4]

Camp 4: The Presidential Leadership Camp: The final group consists of those who see the framers as having invented a limited, republican executive. However, this camp believes that a variety of factors—US superpower status, the age of terrorism, and so on—call for us to reexamine the role, scope, and powers of the presidency in the hope of making the office *both* constitutional *and* powerful.[5]

I embrace the final category. In placing yourself in one of these camps, remember, one must answer two questions: What did the framers intend? What type of presidency does the United States need today? I am convinced that in answer to the first question, the evidence is overwhelming that the framers were indeed antimonarchical, that they rejected the British executive model in favor of a limited executive model under a constitution in which a separation-of-powers framework was intentionally designed to make governing cumbersome. The answer to the second question is more vexing. While aspirationally I am a constitutionalist, my more pragmatic (some might say cynical) side recognizes that it is often a cruel and dangerous world and that there are evil people intent on doing us harm. Thus, I favor a robust yet constitutional presidency, a presidency strong enough to act yet also democratically accountable. I recognize and accept the primacy of presidential leadership in response to crisis or attack. Yet I also see a constructive role for Congress and the courts as potential checks on presidential abuses of power. We cannot simply turn power over to the president and hope for the best.[6]

Having presented the overriding theme of this book, I will proceed to more fully explain how and why we arrived at this juncture and explore ways of dealing with the dilemma of presidential power in a constitutional republic. Chapter 2 takes us back to the invention of the presidency to more clearly discern the goals and sentiments of the framers as they dealt with executive power in the new government. Chapters 3 and 4 trace the rise of presidential power over time. Chapter 5 looks at the impact of 9/11 on presidential power. Chapter 6 looks at different ways of dealing with the problems posed by centralized executive power. Finally, Chapter 7 deals with the presidency as it confronts the challenges of tomorrow.

2

In the Beginning

INVENTING THE PRESIDENCY

Where-ever law ends, tyranny begins.
—John Locke, *Second Treatise of Civil Government*

T he framers of the United States Constitution did not write on a clean slate. With them, they brought the baggage of the Old World. It was largely in reaction to that Old World that the framers wrote the Constitution. The Europe from which the American colonists fled was governed by kings and queens. Monarchies, hereditary governments, and one-man rule characterized Europe, and while the era of the divine right of kings was waning, the remnants of arbitrary and unitary rule remained. The age of the divine right of kings, where the Crown claimed to govern as God's representative on earth, was an era of nearly absolute rule. The king was lawmaker, law interpreter, and law implementer.

While the idea of democracy, consent of the governed, and social contracts were percolating from below, at the dawn of the American Revolution, *democracy* was still a dirty word. Because democracies seem so ubiquitous today, one might mistakenly conclude that a democratic government was the hope and goal of peoples always and everywhere. Not so. It is only in the past 150 years that democracies became established and viable political systems, and only in the past 20 years has democracy spread across the globe. In the 1770s, democracy was still viewed by most influential thinkers as dangerous, leading to mob rule (mobocracy) and rule by the unwashed and uneducated.

Planting the Seeds of Independence

The desire to establish a political democracy was not paramount in the minds of the early settlers of the Americas. They left a Europe of royal rule, rife with religious conflict and persecution, a rigid economic caste system, and a lack of political rights. Democracy was not on the "radar screens" of the early settlers because they were largely unfamiliar with the practices, procedures, language, and structures of democracy.

It was not long, however, before the practice of self-government evolved into a set of experiences and expectations that would lead to demands for political rights and added power for the people to control their own destiny. Nascent forms of self-government emerged in the New World as early as 1607 with the Jamestown, Virginia, settlement. Shortly thereafter, the Pilgrims who landed in Plymouth in 1620 crafted the Mayflower Compact of rights and duties, a compact (social contract) akin to an early constitutional order. As the colonies developed, constitutions with elected assemblies were established to engage the colonists in practices resembling rudimentary forms of political democracy. Such early efforts at self-government could never lose sight of one essential fact: they lived under British rule and were subject to the will of a king. Over time, the tensions between the emerging democratic temperament and the arbitrary power of the king led to open conflicts.

Initially, the colonists' goal was not to revolt against Britain but to become a full-fledged part of Great Britain, ending their colonial status with hopes of becoming fully enfranchised British subjects. But the British still held an impression of the early colonists as criminals, religious fanatics, debtors, ne'er-do-wells, and social outcasts. What may have been partially true at one time, 150 years earlier, no longer reflected the reality in the colonies. Yet, the British refused to recognize the claims of the colonies, and over time pressures built up that would lead to a stark choice for the colonists: subjugation or revolution.[1]

In 1774, with pressure mounting to break from Great Britain, the colonies established the Continental Congress. Its first meeting was in Philadelphia from September 5 to October 26; its goal was to *settle* the dispute with Britain, not separate from the motherland. The congress passed resolutions aimed at gaining certain political and economic rights and presented those requests to the king. But King George III stubbornly refused to grant the requests from the colonists. The colonies then agreed to form another congress, but on April 19, 1775, before it met, fighting broke out at Lexington and Concord in Massachusetts between colonial minutemen and British troops. It became known as "the shot heard 'round the world." Eight minutemen were killed. This further inflamed the passions of the colonists and put pressure on the Continental Congress to become bolder. When the new Continental Congress met on May 10, 1775, the delegates leaned toward revolution. George Washington was named commander of the militia, and war seemed a distinct possibility.

The British Monarchy

In the 1770s, when the colonists looked to the motherland, they saw rule by a powerful, arbitrary monarch. In truth, the days of the all-powerful king had already given way to more balanced and shared power between the monarch and Parliament. And while this form of mixed government was already visibly in the process of politically neutering the English monarchy, the American framers continued to rail against the centralized, arbitrary, and capricious power of a seemingly all-powerful king. It was a convenient, even a necessary, target.

To the colonists, King George III of England was the tyrant against whom any and all charges could be leveled. All revolutions need visible and proximate enemies. To enflame the passion of the people, it is not uncommon to invest all forms of evil in one person. Although this may be a caricature of reality, it is nonetheless a valuable reduction of complex reality into a simplistic, singular enemy. In both the Gulf War of 1990 and later the 2003 war in Iraq, the two President Bushes portrayed Saddam Hussein as "Hitler." This depiction of the potential enemy as the epitome of evil served a powerful purpose: it reduced all evil onto one man and highlighted this evil as the enemy.

A similar process was at work against George III. The colonists dumped all their feelings, all their fears, and all their anger onto one man, the identifiable monster, and monsters had to be destroyed. The dehumanization of George III was but a start, something to fight *against*. They also needed something to fight *for*.

Thomas Paine's *Common Sense*

He had arrived in the colonies from England a mere fourteen months before the January 10, 1776, publication of his influential pamphlet *Common Sense*, but Thomas Paine was, even prior to setting foot in the New World, a rebel, an American patriot, a promoter of liberty, and an enemy of tyranny. Upon publication, *Common Sense* was an instant sensation. It sold a half-million copies and went through twenty-five editions in its first year alone. For a country of about 3 million people, this is remarkable. Its ideas were widely embraced by the colonists, and its message spread like wildfire. According to Scott Liell, "In a relative blink of an eye the spirit of reconciliation would modulate into a passion for independence." And Thomas Paine supplied the prose that led to the passion. Liell continued, "Within the space of a few short months during the winter and spring of 1776, *Common Sense* accomplished what even the bloodshed at Lexington and Concord could not—a wholesale annihilation of the emotional and intellectual ties that bound the American colonists to the British crown and country."[2]

Paine railed against the British monarchy and George III as the "Royal Brute" of Britain and a "crowned ruffian." Paine demonized royalty and focused all blame on the shoulders of the monarch. His assault on the Crown proved one of his most important contributions to the revolutionary cause, as he skewered the very idea of hereditary government and the monarchical pretenses on which it rested.

Thomas Jefferson's Declaration of Independence

Last-ditch efforts to repair the breach with Britain failed, and on July 2, 1776, the Continental Congress "resolved that these United Colonies are, and, of right, ought to be free and independent states." A committee was formed to draft a formal declaration, and the thirty-three-year-old Thomas Jefferson was asked to pen the first draft.

Writing in his personal diary entry dated July 4, 1776, King George III of England wrote, "Nothing of importance on this day."[3] Nothing of importance? July 4, 1776, of course marks the day the framers formally declared their independence from Great Britain. It was a monumental day and a monumental event.

How could one read the powerful words of the Declaration of Independence and not be moved by the sheer force and drama of Jefferson's words? The burst of democratic sentiment, the appeal to reason, the bold language and even bolder message, the call to arms, the proclamation of universal rights, and the condemnation of executive tyranny leave the reader reeling with democratic fervor. From the preamble to the last ringing words, the men of the founding era were truly men for the ages. The preamble reads:

> When, in the course of human events, it becomes necessary for one people to dissolve the political bands which have connected them with another, and to assume among the powers of the earth, the separate and equal station to which the laws of nature and nature's God entitle them, a decent respect to the opinions of mankind requires that they should declare the causes which impel them to separation.

Yet that was only the beginning. Yes, Jefferson wrote, we are breaking our bond with the past, but it is because we believe in certain "universal truths":

> We hold these truths to be self-evident; that all men are created equal, that they are endowed by their Creator with certain unalienable rights, that among these are life, liberty, and the pursuit of happiness.
>
> That, to secure these rights, governments are instituted among men, deriving their just powers from the consent of the governed.
>
> That whenever any form of government becomes destructive of these ends, it is the right of the people to alter or to abolish it, and to institute new government in such form, as to them shall seem most likely to effect their safety and happiness. Prudence, indeed will dictate that governments long established should not be changed for light and transient causes; and accordingly all experience hath shown that mankind are more disposed to suffer while evils are sufferable, than to right themselves by abolishing the forms to which they are accustomed. But when a long train of abuses and usurpations, pursuing invariably the same object,

evinces a design to reduce them under absolute despotism, it is their right, it is their duty, to throw off such government, and to provide new guards for their future security.

Jefferson's language is clear, concise, and direct and oozes both powerful prose and evocative imagery. These inspiring words declare enduring principles as well as independence for a new nation. To further drive home the point, the remainder of the Declaration of Independence is an exhaustive list of crimes and grievances leveled against the British Crown. This bill of particulars includes the following:

> Repeated injuries and usurpations . . .
>
> He has refused his assent to laws . . .
>
> He has obstructed the administration of justice . . .
>
> He has erected a multitude of new offices and sent hither swarms of officers to harass our people and eat their substance . . .
>
> He has affected to render the military independent of, and superior to, the civil power . . .
>
> He has combined with others to subject us to jurisdiction foreign to our constitution and unacknowledged by our laws . . .
>
> For depriving us, in many cases, of benefits of trial by jury . . .
>
> For taking away our charters, abolishing our most valuable laws, and altering, fundamentally, the forms of our government.

Much of this sounds eerily familiar in our age. And although no one would make the case that we have formally replaced an English king with an American one, the ubiquitous presence of the American presidency, the pernicious growth of presidential power in the modern era, and the claims of power made by the George W. Bush administration lead one to draw disturbing parallels.

Jefferson's Declaration was an out-and-out assault against executive tyranny. Following up as it did Paine's *Common Sense*, this two-barreled attack against royalty cemented both the revolutionary commitment of the colonists and the hatred for the monarchy that was so boldly expressed in the Declaration. However, the antiexecutive sentiments, so much a part of the revolutionary rhetoric, would later make it difficult for the framers to construct a government after the Revolution was won.

You Say You Want a Revolution?

Declaring independence was one thing, defeating the world's mightiest military power quite another. Yet, as outlandish as it seems, the colonists did defeat the British, bringing about the independence for which they so hungered. Now came the difficult part: converting their high-minded rhetoric into a workable form of government. The Revolution was fought for the ideas and principles contained in the Declaration of Independence. The framers opposed tyranny, loved liberty, and believed in political equality. How does one make that the basis of government? The framers' first attempt was the Articles of Confederation and Perpetual Union. Written in 1777 by the Continental Congress that had the year before declared independence, the Articles established a "firm league of friendship" among the thirteen colonies/states.

After fighting a revolution against centralized government under a powerful king, it should come as no surprise that the framers created almost a polar opposite of the British state. Instead of a strong central government, the Articles created a weak federal government. The states were quasi independent, and each state retained its "sovereignty, freedom, and independence."

If the framers feared a strong central government, they no less feared a tyrannical monarch. In fact, so antiexecutive were the framers that when they constructed their new government under the Articles, *no executive office was created.* While we can, with perfect twenty-

twenty hindsight, see that such a government would be unworkable, it is important for us to remember that the colonists had just ended a bloody revolution *against* executive government. If they erred too much in the opposite direction, it is entirely understandable.

The Articles worked poorly. The federal government was too weak, the states too strong and independent. It was not long before there was widespread recognition that a stronger central government was necessary and that this new government needed an executive.

The Art of Invention

In the Revolutionary era, the invention of the American presidency began with the destruction of monarchy. Whereas at one time the executive (in the form of monarchy) was seen as the *solution to the problem* (e.g., Machiavelli's Prince was to establish order to the warring Italian city-states), by the mid-1770s, in the American colonies and elsewhere, the executive was increasingly seen as the *problem to be solved*.

The executive was stripped of the patina of legitimacy and transformed into the enemy of the people. Thus, when it came time to create a new government, respect for the executive was at its lowest ebb. The original government under the Articles of Confederation contained *no* executive, with the Continental Congress responsible for all executive functions (often through committees) and later setting up "departments" to conduct business. But with the neutering of the executive complete, the new nation found itself ill-served by this highly decentralized, executiveless government. Having obliterated the executive, how would they resurrect one?

The Revolution against Great Britain was largely a revolution against executive authority. It is difficult to convey to the modern reader just how deep the antipathy to monarchy was in the new nation. Most state constitutions written at this time politically neutered their governors, usually allowing them to serve but one year, granting them little power, and often allowing the state legislature to select the governor. It was a recipe for legislative government. Historian Bernard Bailyn says the rebellion against Britain made resistance to authority "a doctrine according to godliness."[4] The colonists were for the most part fiercely independent, egalitarian, and individualistic. The symbols and rallying cries were antiauthoritarian, and when it became necessary to establish a new government, it was difficult to reestablish the respect for the executive authority so necessary for building effective government.

Reconstructing executive authority was a slow process. By 1787, when the framers met in Philadelphia "for the sole and express purpose of revising the Articles of Confederation . . . [in order to] render the federal constitution adequate to the exigencies of government and the preservation of the Union," there was agreement that a limited executive was necessary to promote good government. But what kind of executive? One person or several? How should he be selected? For how long a term? And with what powers? The framers knew what they did not want; less clear was what they did want in this new executive.[5]

The new nation was so obsessed with the fear that the delegates to the Constitutional Convention were plotting to create an American monarchy that a rumor spread that a "foreign prince" (Frederic, Duke of York, the second son of King George III, was often mentioned) was being brought to America to be made the new king. This rumor got so heated that the delegates felt compelled to lift the agreed-upon veil of secrecy imposed on their proceedings and give assurances to the *Philadelphia Journal*, on August 22: "We are informed that many letters have been written to the members of the Federal convention from different quarters, respecting reports idly circulating that it is intended to establish a monarchical government, to send for [Frederick] &c.— to which it had been uniformly answered, though we cannot affirmatively tell you what we are doing, we can, negatively, tell you what we are not doing—we never once thought of a king."[6] For the framers, no decision was more difficult to reach than the scope and nature of the executive and its powers. The delegates went through proposals, counterproposals, decisions, reconsiderations, postponements, and reversals, until, eventually, a presidency was invented.[7]

Initially, most delegates considered themselves "congressionalists," hoping to create a government with a strong congress and a plural executive with limited power. Delegate George Mason proposed a three-person executive, one chosen from each region of the nation. Delegate Roger Sherman, noting the limited scope of this office, described the executive as "no more than an institution for carrying the will of legislature into effect."

There were, however, a few advocates for a strong, unitary executive. Initially, Alexander Hamilton hoped to create an American version of the British system of government But, there was no support for his proposal, and Hamilton quickly backed away.

James Madison, who is often referred to as the father of the US Constitution, had little impact on the invention of the presidency, going so far as to write in a letter to George Washington shortly before the convention: "I have scarcely ventured as yet to form my own opinion on either of the manner in which [the executive] ought to be constituted or of the authorities with which it ought to be clothed."

Perhaps the most influential framer on the invention of the presidency was James Wilson of Pennsylvania. Initially, Wilson sought the direct, popular election of the president but lost that battle and instead helped develop what became the Electoral College. He also greatly influenced the choice of a single over a plural executive.

In the end, the framers hoped to strike a balance in executive power. Making the presidency too strong would jeopardize liberty; making the office too weak would jeopardize good government. Yet how to achieve balance remained a thorny question.

Unlike the Congress and the judiciary, for which there were ample precedents to guide the framers, the presidency would be a truly new institution, different from any executive office that preceded it. This president would not be a king; he would not be a sovereign. He would swear to protect and defend a higher authority: a constitution.

The thorniest issue confronting the framers was how much power to give this new president. In a way, the framers deftly sidestepped the issue. As they could not reach a consensus on the president's power, they decided to create a bare skeleton of authority, leaving some areas vague and ambiguous; they left gaping silences sprinkled throughout Article II. How could the framers, so afraid of the tyranny of monarchy, leave so important an issue so poorly resolved? The answer is George Washington. Each day the delegates in Philadelphia looked at the man presiding over the convention, secure in the knowledge that whatever else became of this new presidency, George Washington would be the office's first occupant. So confident were the framers in Washington's integrity and republican sentiments, they felt comfortable leaving the presidency unfinished and incomplete. It would be left to George Washington to fill in the gaps and set the proper precedents.

The problem was, of course, that Washington would not always be the president. Thus, although the framers trusted Washington, could they trust his successors? Leaving the presidency unfinished opened the door for future problems in the executive. Benjamin Franklin warned of this when he noted, "The first man, put at the helm, will be a good one. Nobody knows what sort may come afterwards." The presidency that emerged from the Philadelphia convention was an office with "very little plainly given, very little clearly withheld. . . . [T]he Convention . . . did not define: it deferred."[8]

Thus, the presidency would largely be shaped, defined, and created by the people who occupied the office and the demands of different times. The framers invented a "personal presidency," and much of the history of presidential power results from the way individual presidents have understood and attempted to use the office to attain their goals. As Alan Wolfe has written, "The American presidency has been a product of practice, not theory. Concrete struggles between economic and political forces have been responsible for shaping it, not maxims from Montesquieu."[9]

The unsettled nature of the presidential power was a marked characteristic of this peculiar office and, to some, may have marked the genius of the framers. Yet, to others, it was their tragic legacy. The constitution that emerged from the Philadelphia convention was a series of compromise and was less an act of clear design and intent and more a "mosaic of everyone's second choices."[10]

The Constitutional Presidency

The framers invented a republican presidency of some strength, yet possessing little independent power.[11] Article I deals with Congress, which is constitutionally the most powerful branch of government. Most of the powers of the federal government as enumerated in Article I belong to Congress: the power to tax, regulate commerce, declare war, raise armies, and borrow and coin money; all legislative power; and impeachment authority. In addition, the Senate must give its consent to many of the president's appointments. By contrast, Article II, dealing with the presidency, gives the executive few independent powers. Most of the president's powers are shared with Congress. This reflects the ongoing fears of executive tyranny harbored by the framers. They created a circumscribed presidency, not a dominant institution; a republican presidency, not a monarchical office.

In this sense, the presidency was created not as a servant of the Congress but as a semiautonomous institution that possessed some powers independent of Congress, yet most of its powers were shared *with* Congress. A model of concurrent authority and joint decision making was created in the Constitution. Justice Robert Jackson was correct when he wrote that the Constitution "enjoins upon its branches not separateness but interdependence, not autonomy but reciprocity."[12]

A System with Three Parts

We cannot understand the presidency if we do not see the executive connected to the other parts of government. Ours is a *shared* model of power that requires some measure of consensus and cooperation for the government to run smoothly. This Madisonian design necessitates a government of consensus, coalition, and cooperation, on the one hand, and checks, vetoes, and balances on the other.

The primary mechanisms the framers created to control as well as to empower the new government executive are as follows:

1. *Limited government* (a reaction against the arbitrary powers of the king or state and a protection of personal liberty)
2. *Rule of law* (so that only on the basis of law could the government legitimately act)
3. *Separations of powers* (so that the three branches would each have a defined sphere of power)
4. *Checks and balances* (so that each branch could limit or control the powers of the other branches)

Left strictly to its own devices, the presidency is a rather weak, in some way politically anemic, institution. The framers did not make it easy for the government to act or for presidents to dominate (that was clearly not their intent), and they left the powers and controls of the office somewhat vague and ambiguous. Thus, constitutional scholar Edward S. Corwin refers to the new government (referring specifically to foreign policy powers) as "an invitation to struggle" for control of the government.[13] Looking at the framers' design of government, a modern efficiency expert would conclude that the system simply could not work: too many limits, too many checks; not enough power, not enough leadership.

The president has but a few independent powers, and many shared powers, and most are shared with a Congress that has greater constitutional powers but less of an institutional capacity to act. The framers intentionally created uncertainty regarding who holds power in the United States. A system of cross-powers and checked powers created a constitutional mechanism designed to prevent one branch from exercising too much unilateral power. Opportunities to check power abound; opportunities to exercise power are limited. Political scientist Bert Rockman offers this reminder:

> The architect designed many doors, each seemingly with a different lock. In normal times, there would be more locks than keys. Without the intervention of war (and, since Korea, even then) or the appearance of crisis, or the preponderance of like-minded majorities, the independence of institutions so greatly valued by Madison is conducive to the grinding, rather then meshing, of gears. . . . What emerges is not "a government," but many, often competitive and sometimes cooperative, governments; not a decisive point of decision making at the center, but a diffusion of decisional points; and not a state presumably representing a "common and durable interest," but a society whose abundant pluralism finds ready expression through the many conduits available in the polity.[14]

The intent of the framers is clear, and one must remember that this system of separation of powers and checks and balances was designated to prevent tyranny, not promote efficiency. And by these standards, it has worked quite well. At times, the natural lethargy built into the system threatens to grind to a halt. The failure of government to govern, to act, to solve problems is sometimes so overpowering that the fundamental legitimacy of the system seems threatened. Yet it is a system that has largely escaped the crisis of executive tyranny. This fluidity and fragmentation of power create a situation in which "the government" is controlled not by any single person or institution but by different people in different places at different times, sometimes seeking different ends. Although noting that there is, in a technical sense, "a government," Rockman concludes:

> There is not unified government, no government of the day in the modern sense of that term. Instead, the designed of the separation of powers system is predicated on the view expressed by Madison in *Federalist 51* that such a system is essential for the maintenance of liberty. . . . The result is a government founded on defensiveness. Each of its parts can be assertive, but the assertiveness of the parts makes for an unassertiveness of the whole. . . . In short, the system of separated powers was (and largely remains) an institutional design meant to frustrate the exercise of power. This is so because American institutions do not so much divide powers as they divide power. In Samuel Huntington's well-turned sentence, "America perpetuated a fusion of function and a division of power, while Europe developed a differentiation of functions and a centralization of power." Clearly, whatever the virtues of these antique institutions, their strong suite is not the efficient direction of an active government.[15]

Often, the contemporary debate over the framers' view of presidential power is couched as a Hamilton versus Jefferson debate, with Alexander Hamilton favoring a powerful presidency heading a powerful central government and Thomas Jefferson advocating a weak presidency and a weak federal government. Such a distinction, while conceptually useful, does violence to the views of both Hamilton *and* Jefferson.

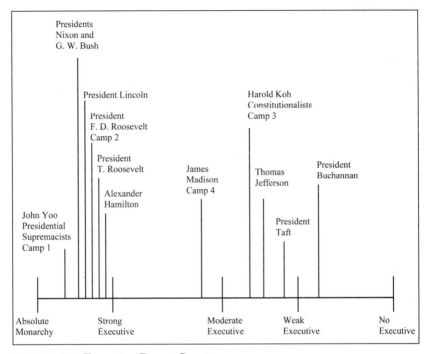

FIGURE 2.1 Executive Power Continuum

Although Hamilton did support an "energetic" executive, he also—especially in *The Federalist Papers* (Nos. 67–77)—supported the presidency as a "republican" office and as *part* of the separation-of-powers system. Some writers take Hamilton's call for "energy in the executive" and extrapolate from it—incorrectly—that energy means unilateral, independent power and dominance similar to the monarchical powers against which the colonists fought a revolution and that the Congress has but a few ways to check presidential power.[16] By the same token, weak executive advocates have also hijacked Thomas Jefferson, who, while calling for government closer to the people and a limited presidency, nonetheless saw times when the executive was compelled to act, even at times beyond the strict limits of the law.[17] (See Figure 2.1.)

As testimony to the framers' reticence to establish an executive with "independent" energy, or a government built for swift action, one need look no further than the separation of powers—a clear indication of the framers' desire to prevent tyranny, *not* promote efficiency in government. The monarchy they had just rebelled against was "efficient." Their new government was designed for prudence, not action. Witness the framers' creation of dual separation, with both *horizontal* separation (the traditional executive-legislative-judicial divide) and *vertical* separation (federalism).

Understanding the Constitution: *The Federalist Papers*

The invention of the presidency was but one step in the creation process. The new system of government still had to be ratified by the states. And one of the chief bones of contention was the presidency and the fear that this new president might become a king. Two opposing camps quickly formed: the *Federalists*, who supported ratification, and the *Anti-Federalists*, most of whom sought a more democratic and decentralized government. It was the Anti-Federalists who were most suspicious of the potential threat of presidential power.

Alexander Hamilton, James Madison, and John Jay began writing newspaper pieces in support of the new Constitution (these would later become *The Federalist Papers*), being careful to note the limits on presidential power. The Anti-Federalists raised their own concerns about the presidency. Edmund Randolph of Virginia said the presidency could be "the fetus of monarchy," George Mason saw the presidency as an "elective monarchy," and Patrick Henry thought the new presidency "squints toward monarchy." They were serious charges and had to be answered.

Hamilton's answer to the Anti-Federalist charges, *The Federalist*, No. 69, is a direct comparison between the newly created president and the king of England and is worth quoting at length:

The president of the United States would be an officer elected by the people for *four* years; the King of Great Britain is a perpetual and *hereditary* prince. The one would be amenable to personal punishment and disgrace [through impeachment]; the person of the other is . . . inviolable. The one would have a *qualified* negative upon the acts of the legislative body; the other has an *absolute* negative. The one would have a right to command the military and naval forces of the nation; the other, in addition to the right, possesses that of *declaring war* [a right reserved to congress in the Constitution], and of *raising* and *regulating* fleets and armies [likewise, a responsibility of Congress] by his own authority. The one would have a concurrent power [with the Senate] in the formation of treaties; the other is the *sole possessor* of the power of making treaties. The one would have a like concurrent authority in appoint to office; the other is the *sole author* of all appointments. The one can confer no privileges whatsoever; the other can make denizens aliens, nobleman commoners; can erect corporations with the rights incident to corporate bodies. The one can prescribe no rules concerning the commerce of currency of the nation; the other is in several respects the arbiter of commerce. . . . The one has no particle of spiritual jurisdiction; the other is supreme head and governor of the national church! What answer shall we give to those who would persuade us that things so unlike resemble each other? The same that ought to be given to those who tell us that a government, the sole power of which would be in the hands of the elective and periodical servants of the people, is an aristocracy, a monarchy, and despotism.

While Hamilton called for an energetic executive, it was an office of inferior power to the British monarch and connected to the other branches by certain checks and balances. Hamilton's energetic executive was a *republican* executive and was part of a larger three-branch form of government.

Other framers expressed concern about this newly created presidency. Thomas Jefferson, writing from Paris to John Adams about the new Constitution, noted that he found "things in it which stagger all my disposition to subscribe to what such an assembly has proposed." Most disturbing to Jefferson was that the presidency reminded him of "a bad edition of a Polish king." As Jefferson reasoned:

> He may be elected 4 years to 4 years for life. Reason and experience prove to us that a chief magistrate, so continuable, is an officer for life. When one or two generations shall have proved that this is an office for life, it becomes on every succession worthy of intrigue, of bribery, of force, and even of foreign interference. . . . Once in office, and possessing the military force of the union, without either the aid or Check of a council, he would not be easily dethroned, even if the people could be induced to withdraw their votes from him.[18]

Despite serious reservation surrounding the presidency, the Constitution was ratified and a presidency created. How well—or poorly—did this new republican executive work?

3

The Rise of Presidential Power

FROM CHIEF CLERK TO LEADER IN WAR, 1787–1865

While the Constitution invented the outline of the American presidency and George Washington operationalized its incomplete creation, history and experience would more fully form this elastic institution.[1] Over time, the presidency would evolve from chief clerk to chief executive to national leader to Imperial President. The modern presidency is less an outgrowth of the constitutional design of the office and more a reflection of ambitious men, demanding times, exploited opportunities, and changed economic and international circumstances.

Was the growth of presidential power inevitable? Political scientists Theodore Lowi and Benjamin Ginsberg see the development of the presidency as "a tug of war between formal constitutional provisions favoring a chief clerk president and a theory of necessity favoring a chief executive president has persisted for two centuries. . . . But it was not until Franklin Roosevelt that the tug of war seems to have been won for the chief executive presidency, because after FDR . . . every president was strong whether he was committed to the strong presidency or not."[2]

Opportunity and *necessity*: two words that will describe why, over time, the power of the presidency expanded. The ambiguities in the original design created opportunities for ambitious men, especially in times of necessity, to increase presidential power. The presidency—elastic, adaptable, even chameleon-like—has been able to transform itself to meet what the times needed, what ambitious presidents grabbed for, what Congress and the courts ceded, what the people wanted, and what world events and American power dictated.

Yet, in other ways, the rise of presidential power is a surprise. It was not supposed to have happened. In strictly constitutional terms, the presidency is a limited office. The United States made the long march from an antiexecutive bias (Revolution) to no executive (Articles) to limited executive (the Constitution) to today. The presidency has not been one thing, but many. And presidential power has not been static, but dynamic.

The American presidency is a complex, multidimensional, paradoxical office.[3] And it is embedded in a *system*—the separation of powers—that intentionally limits the exercise of power. The office has been occupied by *individuals* from a wide range of backgrounds, possessing varied skills, motives, goals, and ambitions. They served under dramatically different conditions and circumstances and at all times are supposed to be guided by the rule of law expressed in the Constitution. It should not then surprise us that the history of the presidency reflects the rise and fall and ebb and flow of political power.

The office of the presidency has been shaped by various individuals, operating within a dynamic system under changing circumstances. Some presidents have been strong, others weak. Some eras demand change; others defy it. The presidency has been shaped by industrialization, the Cold War, American superpower status, economic booms and busts, wars and demands for racial change, increasing democratization, globalization, 9/11, and the demands of capitalism. Presidents helped shape some of these changes, were vic-

TABLE 3.1 Executive Fluctuations in America

Time	Description	Condition
1750–1770	Antiexecutive	Versus Crown
1770–1787	No executive	Articles of Confederation
1787–1820	Limited executive	Constitution
1820–1830	Democratic executive	Jacksonian era
1830–1860	Reaction against executive	Congressional government
1860–1870	Executive emergencies	Lincoln and the Civil War
1860–1888	Reaction against executive	Congressional government
1888–1920	America enters the world	McKinley to Wilson
1920–1932	Reaction against executive	Congressional government
1932–1945	Heroic presidency	FDR, the New Deal, and World War II
1945–1970	National security state	Cold War presidency
1970–1988	Antipresidency	Imperial presidency
1988–2001	Divided and divisive	Post–Cold War presidency
2001–	Antiterrorist era	Imperial presidency

tims of others, and innocent or helpless bystanders in still others. Great social movements, technological changes, newly emergent groups, and a host of other factors created opportunities and restraints on presidential leadership. The story of the rise and fall of presidential power is thus a complex and perplexing one. It is a story of elasticity and adaptability, of leadership and clerkship, of strong and weak officeholders, of change and stasis.

The Expanding Arsenal

The growth of presidential power has occurred in fits and starts. Opportunities and aggressive presidents contributed to the expansion of presidential power, but strong presidents were often followed by a reassertion of congressional authority, leading to a zigzag growth of power over time. But if strong presidents caused a congressional reaction, they left in their wake new tools, new powers, new precedents that over time could be reemployed when opportunities presented themselves and assertive presidents occupied the office. (See Table 3.1.)

What are the key factors that have contributed to the overall expansion of presidential power over time?

First of all, *constitutional ambiguity*: The sometimes vague language of Article II of the US Constitution has served as an open door for some presidents to assert an expansive view of presidential power.

Second, *aggressive presidents*: Some assertive individuals have acted boldly and grabbed power.

Third, *a compliant Congress*: Congress has often been a willing accomplice in its own downfall by either delegating authority to the presidents (e.g., the budget power) or by turning a blind eye as presidents grabbed unprotected powers (e.g., the authority to initiate war and military operations).

Fourth, *crisis and wars*: Crisis and wars have added to the centralization of power in the hands of the presidency.

Fifth, *external threats*: Threats such as Cold War and terrorism have placed greater authority in the hands of presidents.

Sixth, *public demands*: The public has often served as enabler of presidential assertions of power.

Seventh, *a reluctant court*: The courts have been spotty in their efforts to curb the growth of presidential power.

Eighth, the rise of the *welfare state*: With the New Deal, the federal government and the presidency expanded the scope of their involvement in domestic and economic policy.

Ninth, the *administrative presidency*: The expansion of government into social welfare and national defense led to the development of a large bureaucratic structure under the (partial) control of the president.

Tenth, *technology*: The rise in communication technology allowed the presidency to move to center stage and capture the attention of the public. Technology (e.g., nuclear weapons) further centralized power under the control of the presidency.

Eleventh, *globalization*: The rise of globalization has made presidential international deal making more important.

Twelfth, *modernization*: In all industrial democracies, executives are rising in power and legislatures are declining. Modernization makes streamlined executive decision making more important.

Thirteenth, *structure*: Organized as a unitary office, the presidency is structured to move quickly, giving it an *adaptation capability*. Congress, cumbersome and slow to move, is poorly structured for decision making in a fast-paced world. It suffers from an *adaptation crisis*. Presidents can thus initiate action, and Congress can do little but react.

Fourteenth, the emergence of the *national security state* (1940s) and later the *antiterrorism state*: First the Cold War and then the war against terrorism led to the development of a military-industrial complex, the rise of secrecy, and the rise of covert actions, all under the control of the president.

And finally, *the rise of US power*: The rise of US power in economic, military, and hegemonic terms has placed greater power at the disposal of the presidency. The rise of American power has also meant the rise of presidential power. When the United States became a world economic and political power, a strong presidency emerged. With World War II, the Cold War, and now the war against terrorism, the modern presidency has been driven by and shaped by crises and war. With the United States as the world's only superpower, foreign policy animates and empowers a swollen presidency. Yet this powerful and heroic model of the presidency runs contrary to constitutional design. The presidency was invented as a limited institution, grounded by the rule of law and embedded in the checks and balances of a separation of powers. Crises, wars, and international leadership have not changed the wording of the Constitution, but they have altered the scope of presidential power.

This book is about presidential power in an age of US hegemony. It asks if the presidency has become dangerous to our constitutional republic. This concern is not new. James Madison issued a warning more than two hundred years ago when he wrote, "Perhaps it is a universal truth that the loss of liberty at home is to be charged to provisions against danger, real or pretended, from abroad."[4]

As we go abroad in search of demons to destroy, we also sacrifice republican principles at home. As we demand security, we suspend the Constitution. Why give terrorists such a victory they could never earn on the battlefield? Why let thugs and bullies dictate to us? Why do such violence to the Constitution? The current surrendering of our constitutional safeguards is not altogether new. In past wars, we have trimmed the provisions of the Constitution to suit perceived needs and interests. But what is new is the current justification of this constitution smashing.

In effect, we today find ourselves at the third stage of a dangerous trend. In stage one, from the beginning of the Republic to 1950, presidents sought power, used power, and at times abused foreign and war-making power. Yet they were always careful to defend their actions not on the basis of constitutional authority but by the doctrine of necessity. Presidents such as Abraham Lincoln during the Civil War and Franklin D. Roosevelt during the Depression and World War II did overstep constitutional bounds, but they never claimed that their actions were grounded in a constitutional grant of power. Rather than cloaking themselves in constitutional powers, they paid homage to the Constitution and the power of Congress. Lincoln, referring to the emergency measure taken early in the Civil War, admitted in a special session message on July 4, 1861, to Congress that his actions, "whether strictly legal or not, were ventured upon under what appeared to be a popular demand and a public necessity; trusting then as now that Congress would readily ratify them."[5] Lincoln made no claim of inherent plenary power and bowed to the superior power of the Constitution, the rule of law, and the right of Congress to make policy. Presidents occasionally have acted beyond the law, but they have been careful never to claim a constitutional "right" to do so.

Stage two came in the early 1950s when, during the early days of the Cold War, President Harry S Truman broke from our constitutional past to assert an inherent right as commander in chief to send US troops into combat during the Korean War. This bold and constitutionally baseless claim should have been defanged at birth, but in the early days of the Cold War, Congress, the public, and the courts backed away, careful not to be accused of being soft on communism, and a new "constitutional" principle was accepted, a principle many subsequent presidents, along with the public, Congress, courts, and the media, began to accept as a legitimate constitutional provision.

We find ourselves today on the precipice of stage three, when President Bush, fighting a war against terrorism, took Truman's constitutionally baseless doctrine one giant step further. Not only did Bush claim an inherent constitutional right to send troops into combat without congressional approval, but he asserted an even more far-fetched and dangerous power: that his actions were nonreviewable.[6] If the Congress, public, and courts allow such an assertion to become doctrine, what becomes of the system of checks and balances? Is the president to be truly above the law? Accepting the Bush interpretation would transform the imperial presidency into a monarchal presidency.

Such is the dilemma we attempt to confront in this book. Is the presidency dangerous to democracy, and what are the challenges we face as we attempt to make the presidency powerful enough to promote security while also maintaining democratic accountability? Can we make the presidency strong *and* safe for democracy?

The growth of presidential power occurred absent any significant changes to the US Constitution. It was primarily the result of opportunities grabbed, needs met, and conditions changed, augmented by determined and assertive presidents pressing for more power in the separated system. With the growth of American power internationally came the simultaneous growth of presidential power. The two were inextricably linked. (See Table 3.2 for a review of each administration.)

How Presidents Contributed to the Growth of the Presidency

The presidency of today is the result of more than two hundred years of development. In fits and starts, resembling a roller-coaster ride, the presidency has grown and shrunk; presidential power has expanded and contracted. However, if the presidency has been the product of these dramatic fluctuations, the overall trend has been toward growth—unsteady and uneven—but growth nonetheless. Some presidents enlarged the office; others diminished it. Some left new tools for their successors to use; others left their successors in seemingly hopeless situations.

Of all the framers' inventions, the presidency was left least formed. Thus, while the office may have been literally invented by the framers, it was more fully brought to life by Washington and his successors. The office cannot be understood solely by an examination of the Constitution. It can only be understood when we examine its historical development. The presidency that emerged from the Philadelphia convention was incomplete. Thus, Washington, the first president, ventured into largely uncharted territory. Virtually everything was new. There was some, but precious little, constitutional guidance. Washington would have to invent an office as he went along. The presidency is an office made in practice as much as one drafted on paper in Philadelphia.

George Washington, who more than anyone else brought the presidency to life by giving operational substance to the words of

TABLE 3.2 Synopsis of Presidential Administrations

President	Party	Political Changes	Cultural and Technological Changes	Achievements	Power Contribution	Rating
George Washington 1789–1797 *President Number 1*	Democratic-Republic	First presidential election (1789) Bill of Rights (1791) Jay Treaty (1794) Creation of two political parties (1790s)	1st Census: U.S. population just under 4 million, including approximately 700,000 slaves and 60,000 free blacks (1790) Cotton gin (1793) Washington, D.C. established as the nation's capital (1790) U.S. Navy (1794) 1st U.S. Opera (1796) 1st Paddle-wheel steamboat (1797)	Set valuable and lasting precedents; "invented," in practice, much of the presidency; nation-building	Independence from Congress Treaty making authority	#3 Above Average
John Adams 1797–1801 *Number 2*	Federalist	Alien and Sedition Acts (1798) Undeclared naval war with France (1798–1800)	Washington becomes US capitol (1800) Library of Congress established (1800)	Avoided major war with France		#9 Above Average

(continues)

TABLE 3.2 *(continued)*

President	Party	Political Changes	Cultural and Technological Changes	Achievements	Power Contribution	Rating
Thomas Jefferson 1801–1809 *Number 3*	Democratic-Republic	War with Tripoli (1801–1805) Louisiana Purchase (1803) Marbury v. Madison (1803) Lewis and Clark Expedition (1804) Congress bans African slave trade (1808)	Gas street lighting introduced (1806) Webster publishes 1st US dictionary (1806) Fulton's steamboat (1807) "America the Beautiful" (1808)	Greatly expanded size of United States (Louisiana Purchase) Peaceful transition from one party rule to another Exerted party leadership	Party leadership Independent action	#4 Great
James Madison 1809–1817 *Number 4*	Democratic-Republic	War of 1812 Treaty of Ghent (1814)	US population more than 7 million (1810) "Uncle Sam" invented (1812) "The Star-Spangled Banner" (1814)	Led nation into unnecessary war		#14 Above Average
James Monroe 1817–1825 *Number 5*	Democratic-Republic	*McCulloch v. Maryland* (1819) Missouri Compromise (1820) Monroe Doctrine (1823)	US flag design established (1818) Irving's "Rip Van Winkle" and "Legend of Sleepy Hollow" (1820) Moore's *'Twas the Night Before Christmas* (1822)	Attained Florida from Spain Created Monroe Doctrine Signed Missouri Compromise	Foreign policy authority	#15 Above Average

President	Party				Ranking
John Quincy Adams 1825–1829 *Number 6*	Democratic-Republic	Democratic Party formed (1828)	Erie Canal opens (1825) 50th anniversary of Declaration of Independence (1826) Cooper's *Last of the Mohicans* (1826) Photographic camera (1826) 1st US ballet (1827) Freedom's Journal, 1st Negro newspaper (1827)		#16 Above Average
Andrew Jackson 1829–1837 *Number 7*	Democrat	Nat Turner Rebellion (1831) Battle over national bank (1830–1832) Whig Party formed (1834) Battle of the Alamo (1836)	US Census places population at 13 million (1830) 1st Anti-Slavery Society (1834) Colt revolver (1835) United States is debt free for first time in history (1836)	Expanded presidential power and linked president to public opinion — Linked presidency with the people	#7 Near Great
Martin Van Buren 1837–1841 *Number 8*	Democrat	Independent Treasury Act (1840)	Morse telegraph (1837) Women given legal control over property (1839) Bicycle invented (1839) First university degrees for women (1841)	Nation entered economic depression	#20 Average

(continues)

TABLE 3.2 (*continued*)

President	Party	Political Changes	Cultural and Technological Changes	Achievements	Power Contribution	Rating
William Henry Harrison 1841 *Number 9*	Whig			Was president for only one month		
John Tyler 1841–1845 *Number 10*	Whig			Established precedent that upon death of president, the vice president becomes president		#29 Below Average
James K. Polk 1845–1849 *Number 11*	Democrat	"Manifest Destiny" (1845) Oregon Treaty (1846) Mexican War (1846–1848)	Poe's "The Raven" (1845) Sewing machine (1846) Smithsonian Institution (1846) Women's Rights Convention (1848) California Gold Rush (1848)	"Forced" a war with Mexico	War initiation	#12 Above Average
Zachary Taylor 1849–1850 *Number 12*	Whig		US Census places population at 23 million (1850)			#27 Below Average

President	Party	Events	Culture/Science	Accomplishments	Ranking
Millard Fillmore 1850–1853 *Number 13*	Whig	Compromise of 1850	*New York Times* (1851) Melville's *Moby Dick* (1851) Elevator (1852) Stowe's *Uncle Tom's Cabin* (1852) Hawthorne's *The Scarlet Letter* (1852)	Opened trade with Japan Great Compromise of 1850	#30 Below Average
Franklin Pierce 1853–1857 *Number 14*	Democrat	Kansas-Nebraska Act (1854) Republican Party formed (1854)	Thoreau's *Walden* (1854) Whitman's *Leaves of Grass* (1855) "Jingle Bells" (1857)	Gadsden purchase	#32 Below Average
James Buchanan 1857–1861 *Number 15*	Democrat	*Dred Scott* v. Sanford (1857) John Brown's raid (1859) South Carolina secedes from Union (1860) Confederate States formed (1861)	Transatlantic telegraph (1858) Darwin's theory of evolution (1859) J. S. Mill's *On Liberty* (1859) Pony Express (1860)	Could not halt the movement to Civil War	#34 Failure
Abraham Lincoln 1861–1865 *Number 16*	Republican	Civil War (1861–1865) Emancipation Proclamation (1863) Assassinated (1865)	"Battle Hymn of the Republic" (1862) Gettysburg Address (1863)	Held nation together through Civil War Freed slaves Crises and war powers	#1 Great

(continues)

TABLE 3.2 (*continued*)

President	Party	Political Changes	Cultural and Technological Changes	Achievements	Power Contribution	Rating
Andrew Johnson 1865–1869 *Number 17*	Republican	Tenure in Office Act (1865) 13th Amendment abolishes slavery (1866) Reconstruction Act (1867) Johnson Impeached but escapes conviction by one vote (1868) 14th Amendment (1868)	Ku Klux Klan formed (1866) Women's Rights Convention (NYC) (1866) Winchester rifle (1866) Alcott's *Little Women* (1866) Alaska Purchase (1866) Alger's *Ragged Dick* (1866) Dynamite (1867) Transcontinental railroad (1869)	Battled with Congress (unsuccessfully) over Reconstruction		#33 Failure
Ulysses S. Grant 1869–1877 *Number 18*	Republican	Wyoming, first state to allow women to vote (1869) 15th Amendment (1870) First blacks in Congress (1870) Civil Rights Act (1874)	Electric chair (1870) US Census places population at nearly 40 million (1870) *Whistler's Mother* (1871) Battle of Little Big Horn (1876) Telephone (1876) Twain's *Tom Sawyer* (1876)	Scandal plagued administration		#36 Failure

President	Party	Legislation	Events	Achievements	Ranking
Rutherford B. Hayes 1877–1881 *Number 19*	Republican	Reconstruction ends (1877) Bland Allison Act (1877)	Knights of Labor formed (1878) Phonograph (1878) Electric light (1879) Salvation Army (1880) US Census places population at more than 50 million (1880)	Ended Reconstruction Civil Service reform efforts	#22 Average
James Garfield 1881 *Number 20*	Republican			Killed early in term	
Chester A. Arthur 1881–1885 *Number 21*	Republican	Pendleton Act (1883)	Red Cross (1881) Statue of Liberty (1883) Washington Monument begun (1884) Twain's *Huckleberry Finn* (1885)	Civil Service reform Modernized Navy	#23 Average
Grover Cleveland 1885–1889 *Number 22*	Democrat	AFL organized (1887)	Geronimo surrenders (1886) Silent motion pictures (1889)	Reform of government	#17 Above Average
Benjamin Harrison 1889–1893 *Number 23*	Democrat	Sherman Anti-Trust Act (1890) Wounded Knee massacre (1890) Populist Party formed (1892)	Basketball invented (1891) Pledge of Allegiance (1892) Gas-powered and electric automobile (1893)	Strong foreign policy Enlarged navy	#26 Average

(continues)

TABLE 3.2 *(continued)*

President	Party	Political Changes	Cultural and Technological Changes	Achievements	Power Contribution	Rating
Grover Cleveland 1893–1897 *Number 24*	Democrat	*Plessy v. Ferguson* (1896)	"America the Beautiful" (1893) Kipling's *Jungle Book* (1894) X-ray (1895) Crane's *Red Badge of Courage* (1895) First modern Olympics (1897)			#23 Average
William McKinley 1897–1901 *Number 25*	Republican	Spanish-American War (1898) Hawaii annexed (1898) Assassinated (1901)	Aspirin (1899) US Census places population at nearly 76 million (1900) Radio (1901) Stock-market collapse (1901)	Pushes into war with Spain Beginning of US "empire" United States becomes a "world power" Acquired Philippines, Hawaii, Guam, and Puerto Rico as US possessions	United States as imperial power	#18 Average

President	Party	Events	Accomplishments	Themes	Ranking
Theodore Roosevelt 1901–1909 *Number 26*	Republican	Trust busting (1902) Panama Canal (1904) Immigration Act (1907) Wright brothers' flight (1903) First World Series (1903) London's *Call of the Wild* (1903) 1st direct blood transfusion (1905) Sinclair's *The Jungle* (1906) Theodore Roosevelt wins Nobel Peace Prize (1906)	Activist president Used "bully pulpit" Expanded presidential power Trust busters National parks Panama Canal	Bully pulpit Cult of personality Foreign policy leadership	#5 Near Great
William Taft 1909–1913 *Number 27*	Republican	1st minimum-wage law (1912) Federal income tax (16th Amendment) (1913) Model T car (1909) Peary reaches North Pole (1909) NAACP established (1910) Boy Scouts and Camp Girls established (1910) US Census places population at 92 million (1910) Pulitzer Prize established (1911)	Conservation of national resources Post office reform Trust buster		#19 Average
Woodrow Wilson 1913–1921 *Number 28*	Democrat	Federal Reserve Act (1913) World War I (1914–1918) Prohibition (18th Amendment) (1920) Women attain the right to vote (19th Amendment) (1920) Panama Canal opens (1914) Einstein's theory of relativity (1915) Chaplin's *The Tramp* (1915) "Red Scare" raids (1920) Submachine gun (1920)	Reformed banking laws Antitrust laws War leadership Promoted League of Nations and "14 Points" Enlarged presidential power	War authority International leadership	#6 Near Great

(continues)

TABLE 3.2 (*continued*)

President	Party	Political Changes	Cultural and Technological Changes	Achievements	Power Contribution	Rating
Warren Harding 1921–1923 *Number 29*	Republican	Naval Arms Limitation Pact (1921)	Insulin (1922) Television (1923) Gershwin's "Rhapsody in Blue" (1923) Sound films (1923)	Weak president Scandal-plagued administration		#37 Failure
Calvin Coolidge 1923–1929 *Number 30*	Republican	Scopes Trial (1925) Kellogg-Briand Pact (1928)	1st presidential radio broadcast (1923) Fitzgerald's *The Great Gatsby* (1925) Frozen food (1925) Scopes monkey trial (1925) Lindbergh crosses the Atlantic in airplane (1927) Stalin gains control of Soviet Union (1928) Penicillin (1929) Mickey Mouse (1929)	Weak president		#31 Below Average
Herbert Hoover 1929–1933 *Number 31*	Republican	Stock-market crash and Great Depression (1929)	Museum of Modern Art (1929) 1st computer (1930) Empire State Building (1931) Huxley's *Brave New World* (1932) 1st woman elected to US Senate (1932)	Unfairly blamed for Depression, helpless in its wake		#21 Average

President	Party	Events	Achievements	Domestic/economic policy authority	Ranking
Franklin D. Roosevelt 1933–1945 *Number 32*	Democrat	New Deal (1933) Social Security (1935) Court Packing Plan (1937) World War II (1939–1945) Lend-lease (1941) Pearl Harbor bombing (1941) Nazis begin systematic extermination of the Jews (1942) Relocation of Japanese Americans (1942) 1st woman appointed to cabinet (1933) Radar (1935) 1st Xerox machine (1938) *Gone with the Wind* (1939) Helicopter (1939) Steinbeck's *Grapes of Wrath* (1939) "God Bless America" (1939) Manhattan Project (1942) *Casablanca* (1942)	Activist president Expanded presidential power Saw nation through two crises	Domestic/economic policy authority War leadership	#2 Great
Harry S Truman 1945–1953 *Number 33*	Democrat	Atomic bomb dropped on Japan (1945) World War II ends (1945) Truman Doctrine (1947) Cold War begins (1947) National Security Act (1947) Marshall Plan (1947) West Berlin airlift (1948) NATO (1949) "Containment" of Soviet Union (1949) Korean War (1950) 1st electronic digital computer (1946) Jackie Robinson, 1st black Major League Baseball player (1947) Supreme Court bans prayer in public schools (1948) Orwell's *1984* (1949) Red Scare/McCarthyism (1950) US Census places population at 150 million (1950) Atomic bomb (1950) Salinger's *The Catcher and the Rye* (1951) Video camera (1951) 1st jet service (1952) Hemingway's *Old Man and the Sea* (1952) H-bomb (1952)	Developed US response to Soviet Union United States becomes leader of free world National security state created	Cold War authority Independent war power	#8 Near Great

(continues)

TABLE 3.2 (*continued*)

President	Party	Political Changes	Cultural and Technological Changes	Achievements	Power Contribution	Rating
Dwight D. Eisenhower 1953–1961 *Number 34*	Republican	War in Korea ends (1953) Civil Rights Act (1957) Troops sent to desegregate Little Rock schools (1957) U-2 shot down (1960)	1st nuclear power plant (1957) Freedom Rights (1961) Berlin Wall (1961)	Returned nation to relative calm after tumultuous years of depression, World War II, and nascent Cold War	Covert operations	#11 Above Average
John F. Kennedy 1961–1963 *Number 35*	Democrat	Bay of Pigs (1961) Peace Corps (1961) Cuban missile crisis (1962) Nuclear Test Ban Treaty (1963) Assassinated (1963)	1st American in space (1961) Heller's *Catch-22* (1961) John Glenn orbits Earth (1962) Martin Luther King Jr. leads civil rights movement (1963)	Peace Corps Cuban missile crisis	Media cultivation	#13 Above Average
Lyndon B. Johnson 1963–1969 *Number 36*	Democrat	Race riots (1960s) Civil Rights Act (1964) Great Society (1964) Voting Rights Act (1965) Medicare (1966) Thurgood Marshall, 1st black in Supreme Court (1967) Martin Luther King Jr. assassinated (1968) Robert Kennedy assassinated (1969)	Martin Luther King Jr. receives Nobel Peace Prize (1964) Antiwar protests (1966–) 1st successful heart transplant (1967)	Major achievements in domestic arena overshadowed by Vietnam	Imperial presidency	#10 Above Average

President	Party	Events	Accomplishments		Ranking
Richard M. Nixon 1969–1974 *Number 37*	Republican	Environmental Protection Agency established (1970) Voting age lowered to 18 (26th Amendment) (1972) Détente (1972) Nixon visits China (1972) Watergate (1972) SALT I (1972) Vice President Agnew resigns (1973) *Roe v. Wade* (1973) Resigns from office (1974)	1st man on the moon (1969) Kent State killings (1970) US Census places population at more than 203 million (1970) OPEC crisis (1973)	Ended war in Vietnam Improved relations with Soviet Union and China Watergate scandal, named unindicted coconspirator, resigned in disgrace	Imperial presidency	#35 Failure
Gerald Ford 1974–1977 *Number 38*	Republican	Ford pardons Nixon (1974) Vietnam War formally ends (1975)		Helped heal wounds of Vietnam and Watergate 1st nonelected president	Imperiled presidency	#24 Average
Jimmy Carter 1977–1981 *Number 39*	Democrat	United States opens formal relations with China (1978) Camp David Accords (1978) Panama Canal Treaty (1978) US-Iran hostage crisis (1979)	United States boycotts Moscow Olympics (1980) US Census places population at 226 million (1980)	Focused on human rights	Imperiled presidency	#25 Average

(continues)

TABLE 3.2 *(continued)*

President	Party	Political Changes	Cultural and Technological Changes	Achievements	Power Contribution	Rating
Ronald Reagan 1981–1989 *Number 40*	Republican	Iran frees US hostages (1981) Assassination attempt (1981) Sandra Day O'Connor 1st woman on Supreme Court (1981) Equal Rights Amendment fails (1982) 241 Marines killed in Beirut bombing (1983) Granada invasion (1983) US mines harbors in Nicaragua (1984) Reagan turns executive power over to Vice President Bush during operation (1985)	AIDS identified (1981) National debt passes $1 trillion	Restored confidence in United States Allowed budget deficit to skyrocket Scandal-plagued administration Iran-Contra scandal (1986) INF Treaty (1987)	Administrative strategy	#28 Below Average
George H. W. Bush 1989–1993 *Number 41*	Republican	Soviet Empire implodes (1989) United States invades Panama (1989) Berlin Wall falls (1989) Persian Gulf War (1991)	Exxon Valdez oil crisis (1989) Los Angeles race riots (1992)	Gulf War End of Cold War Americans with Disabilities Act	Managerial presidency	

President	Party					
Bill Clinton 1993–2001 *Number 42*	Democrat	Dramatically reduced budget deficit; Scandals during administration	World Trade Center bombing (1993); US Census places population at 281.4 million (2000)	Brady Bill; NAFTA; Family Medical Leave Act; Welfare reform; Impeachment hearing	"The Natural"	N/A
George W. Bush (II) 2001–2009 *Number 43*	Republican	September 11, 2001, terrorist attack against United States; War in Afghanistan; War in Iraq; Tax cuts; Budget deficit; Weak dollar; Weakened relations with allies; Curtailed constitutional rights; Economic bust	iPod; Facebook	Created Department of Homeland Security; War against terrorism	Unilateral exercise of power asserted that his actions against terrorism are "nonreviewable" and created "antiterrorism state"	N/A
Barack Obama 2009– *Number 44*	Democrat	Internet campaigning; 1st African American president; Rise of Tea Party movement; Deficit/economic crisis; Libyan air strikes	iPad	Passed economic stimulus package; Wall Street regulation; Health care reform; Ended "Don't Ask, Don't Tell"; Got Bin Laden		N/A

Source: Adapted from Michael A. Genovese, *The Power of the American Presidency* (New York: Oxford University Press, 2000).

the Constitution, contributed to the expansion of presidential power at key points by stretching the constitutional limits of the office. At six foot three, President George Washington (1789–1797) was a towering figure. Beyond his imposing physical presence, Washington was also the towering figure of his era because of his accomplishments, character, and the high esteem in which he was held by his contemporaries. Washington was seen as a man of honor and virtue. He could have been king but chose instead to be president. That alone endeared him to his countrymen.

Washington viewed the American experiment in republican government as hopeful yet fragile. He knew his role in establishing a presidency was of enormous significance. Hoping to establish dignified republican norms and standards, he tried to show by example what was required of the new republican government. When George Washington took the oath of office as the first president in 1789, people had great confidence in him. There were, however, grave doubts about the legitimacy and role of this new office called a "presidency."

The Constitution raised more questions than it answered. Vague and ambiguous, barely charting a skeletal organization for the new office, there was confusion over the political role and character of this office. Article II's opening, "The executive power shall be vested in a President," settled little. What powers? What limits? What relation to Congress, to the courts? What connection to the people?

Ever aware of the importance of each step, act, decision, and nondecision, Washington told James Madison, "As the first of everything, in our situation will serve to establish a precedent, it is devoutly wished on my part, that these precedents may be fixed on true principles. I walk," he noted, "on untrodden ground. There is scarcely any part of my conduct that may not hereafter be drawn into precedent." He further noted, "Many things which appear of little importance in themselves and at the beginning may have great and durable consequences from their having been established at the commencement of a new general government." Here was a man creating an institution step by step as he went along. The Constitution of 1787 was painted in broad strokes. It was left to Washington (and his successors) to fill in the details. This left considerable leeway for Washington to invent an office. He was not handed a blank slate on which to draw, but the ambiguities of the Constitution left room for individuals and events to complete the job the framers had only started.

Virtually every act had meaning, and Washington was able to establish a number of important, even lasting, precedents. One of his key contributions was in wrestling some executive independence from Congress in several important areas. He established a precedent of hiring and firing (the latter a serious bone of contention) a cabinet and key executive officers.

He also attained a modicum of independent control over foreign affairs and treaty making. Negotiations with Native-American tribes put executive-congressional relations to the test early in his administration. The Constitution called for the president to seek advice and consent of the Senate in making treaties, but what form should such advice take? Washington asked James Madison how to proceed. "Would an oral or written communication be best? If first, what mode is to be adopted to affect it?" On August 22, 1789, the president asked the Senate for consultation regarding a proposed treaty. Vice President John Adams read a message to the Senate from President Washington that concerned several points about the treaty, hoping to get the Senate's *advice* and *consent*. A confused Senate, surprised and unprepared to meet Washington's request, could not figure out how to respond. Washington grew progressively impatient, declaring, "This defeats every purpose of my coming here." So put off was Washington that he resolved never again to seek Senate consultation.

In 1791, Washington, influenced by his treasury secretary, Alexander Hamilton, agreed to support the creation of a Bank of the United States, modeled on the Bank of England. Thomas Jefferson, Washington's secretary of state, quickly challenged the bank, asking, "Is it constitutional?" A majority of the president's cabinet had doubts. But Hamilton, arguing that the president, like Congress, had *implied powers* that, while not specified, were derived from the Constitution and necessary for the exercise of governing, won Washington over. The president signed the bank into law, legitimizing the view that the president had certain "implied powers," thereby setting a precedent that further expanded presidential power.

Washington also helped establish what later was to be called "executive privilege." Following a failed military expedition by General Arthur St. Clair, the House of Representatives insisted that the War Department produce documents relating to the expedition. Initially reluctant to turn over the documents, Washington discussed the issue in cabinet and eventually, not only consented to produce the documents, but also sent his secretaries of war and treasury to testify in person before Congress.

Washington was the first president to use the *veto*. The question was: When can a president legitimately exercise the veto? Was it permissible to veto legislation with which one simply disagrees on policy, or can the president only veto legislation he believes is unconstitutional? Initially, Washington was reluctant to use his veto power, but Jefferson, warning the president that if unused, the veto power might atrophy, persuaded Washington to veto a bill on the grounds that it violated the Constitution. During his eight years in office, Washington vetoed only two bills.

What powers did the president possess to respond to a domestic rebellion? This question arose during the Whiskey Rebellion of 1794. Militant opposition to a national excise tax on whiskey production grew increasingly violent. The "rebellion" was especially dangerous in western Pennsylvania. Washington's initial response was to issue a warning, demanding that the rebels "disperse and retire peaceably to their respective abodes," warning "all persons whomsoever against aiding, abetting, or comforting the perpetuators of the . . . treasonable acts." He also called upon the governors of several states to supply a militia force to squelch the rebellion. Troops marched into western Pennsylvania in an impressive show of force, and the rebels dispersed. Two of the rebels were convicted of treason, but Washington, confirming yet another presidential power, pardoned both men. In his response to the Whiskey Rebellion, Washington asserted the supremacy of the federal over state governments and demonstrated that the new government could, and would, enforce the law, by force if necessary.

While the Constitution called for major presidential appointments to the executive branch to receive the "advice and consent" of the Senate, it said nothing of the removal of power. Ultimately, this was a question of who controlled the bureaucracy—the president or Congress. In a 29–22 vote, the House decided to give the president removal power. But that issue would come back to haunt presidents and congresses in future years.

Another seminal event in Washington's presidency revolved around foreign affairs. In 1789, the French Revolution began. However, over time, it went from great promise to tragedy. Two weeks after Washington's second inauguration, King Louis XVI was beheaded, and soon Great Britain was at war with France. American sympathies were divided, with Jefferson and his followers supporting France and Hamilton and his followers supporting Britain. The political and personal cleavages that had been emerging in America threatened to crack into open warfare.

Hoping to avoid further trouble, Washington issued a proclamation of neutrality. But Britain ignored the proclamation and began seizing American ships. Washington, still hoping to avoid a direct conflict, appointed John Jay to negotiate a treaty with Britain. When the terms of the treaty were announced, the Jeffersonians complained that the United States had caved in to almost all of Britain's demands. Yet Washington signed the treaty.

Did the president have the plenary authority to issue a proclamation of US policy? Could the president declare neutrality? A heated debate between Hamilton and Madison took place in the public press. Hamilton, writing under the pseudonym "Pacificus," argued for an expansive view of presidential power, and Madison, writing as "Helvidius," argued that this was an unconstitutional extension of presidential power, a usurpation of congressional authority. Hamilton's position won out, as Washington *did* declare neutrality. This set another important precedent, allowing the president to set policy in foreign affairs, and it led to a more expansive view of the president's implied powers under the Constitution.

In the end, what was Washington's contribution to this new government and this new presidency? Whereas James Madison is rightfully known as the father of the US Constitution, no one contributed more to the operation of the new government than George Washington. It was Washington who put the constitutional framework on solid footing and served when the Bill of Rights was adopted.[7]

The next president to significantly expand the powers of the office was Thomas Jefferson (1801–1809). Thomas Jefferson, author of the Declaration of Independence and third president of the United States, embraced a small-government, rural, Whiggish system that advocated a limited executive. He was suspicious of central authority, and in the Declaration of Independence he railed against the abuses of the Crown and tyranny of the monarchy. Yet, as president, he at times added to the power of the office.

Jefferson wanted to reduce the pomp surrounding the presidency and bring it back to more democratic and republican manners. He did away with bowing, replacing this regal custom with the more democratic handshake. Jefferson abolished the weekly levee, ended formal state dinners, and abandoned Washington's custom of making personal addresses to Congress (this may have been due as much to Jefferson's weak speaking voice as to his republican sentiments). This practice continued until 1913 and the Wilson presidency. Jefferson utilized the cabinet as a powerful instrument of presidential leadership. His cabinet was loyal, experienced, and committed to pushing the president's agenda in Congress.

The president also exerted increased influence over the Congress. Employing the president's power as *party leader*, Jefferson, while respecting the constitutional prerogatives of Congress, nonetheless used a variety of means to press his goals in the legislature. He lobbied key party leaders, drafted bills for his supporters to introduce, authorized key party members to act as his spokesmen in Congress, informally lobbied legislators at social gatherings in the White House, and had cabinet members work closely with Congress. This allowed Jefferson to exert considerable influence over the Congress.

Jefferson's use of political party was an innovation in presidential leadership. It was an exercise of extraconstitutional power, but one necessary to make the Constitution operate effectively. It allowed Jefferson to build a strong presidency, responsive to the majority will of the people, as expressed through the majority political party.

Jefferson also used, with great effect, dinners with legislators as an effective tool of leadership. He would invite congressmen to dinner at the White House two or three times each week when Congress was in session. As Jefferson explained his motives: "I cultivate personal intercourse with the members of the legislature that we may know one another and have opportunities of little explanations of circumstances, which, not understood, might produce jealousies and suspicions injurious to the public interest, which is best promoted by harmony and mutual confidence among its functionaries. I depend much on the members for local information necessary in local matters, as well as for the means of getting at public sentiment."[8]

Jefferson never cast a veto in his two terms as president, and he viewed the veto power quite narrowly, believing it should be reserved only for bills deemed unconstitutional (in fact, in the forty years from 1789 to 1829, a span covering six administrations, only ten presidential vetoes were cast). Given his skilled and activist leadership of Congress, the president never felt compelled to put his views to the test.

Such activist intervention surprised many of Jefferson's Federalist critics, who thought the new president's goal was to limit governmental and presidential power. But undoing the Federalist policies required the use of executive leadership; power was needed to vanquish power, and "the more the President exercised power with righteous purpose, the less scrupulous he became towards abjurations of Republican theory."[9]

If George Washington talked of asserting executive privilege, it was Jefferson who first truly pursued it. Subpoenaed to testify at the treason trial of Vice President Aaron Burr, Jefferson flatly refused to appear. He did, however, release selected documents. This assertion established a precedent that partially insulates the executive branch from intrusions by the legislative and judicial branches.

One of the key dilemmas faced by President Jefferson was what to do about pirates operating against American ships in the Mediterranean. The president ordered a squadron of American fighting ships to sail to the region. "But," Jefferson cautioned, "as this might lead to war, I wished to have the approbation of the new administration."[10] At issue was the question of how much authority the president had to initiate military action. Jefferson's cabinet agreed that the squadron should be sent to the region to protect American shipping, but they were unsure whether the president alone had the authority to order such activity. In the end, Jefferson recognized that the Constitution gave Congress the power to declare war and said that the squadron could engage only in *defensive* actions (a fine line perhaps, yet a line nonetheless). Jefferson defined *defensive* broadly, however. While a powerful constitutional argument, events would, over time, erode this somewhat restrictive view of a president's authority over foreign affairs.

Prior to the presidency, Jefferson penned his famous *Notes on the State of Virginia* (1781, later updated and revised), in which he faulted the US Constitution for not providing a strong-enough separation-of-powers system. "All the powers of the government . . . result to the legislative body."[11] Yes, he also chided those who called for a "dictator" to cope with threats from abroad. He insisted that even temporary dictatorship could not be justified by an argument of "necessity." If Virginia had accepted a dictator, it would have given the nation's enemies a "proof, which they would have trumpeted through the universe, of the inability of republican government, in times of pressing danger." A few years later, when Jefferson revised his *Notes*, he further attempted to define the proper executive for a republic, explicitly denying the governor "prerogative power."[12]

As president, Jefferson changed his tune a bit. An advocate of a narrow construction of the Constitution, Jefferson was confronted with an opportunity to purchase the Louisiana Territory from France. This purchase would more than double the size of the nation and remove a potential rival from the nation's borders. However, there was a problem that Jefferson recognized: the Constitution did not permit him to make the purchase. It was an incredible opportunity to advance the interests of the United States, yet Jefferson was rightly troubled by the fact that it was unconstitutional. Jefferson had a constitutional amendment drafted that would have made the purchase acceptable, but Senator Wilson Cary Nicholas persuaded him not to pursue the amendment. The president remained troubled. In a letter to Nicholas, Jefferson wrote of his lingering doubts: "When an instrument admits two constructions, the one safe, the other dangerous, the one precise, the other indefinite, I prefer that which is safe & precise. I had rather ask an enlargement of power from the nation where it is found necessary than to assume it by a construction which would make our powers boundless. Our peculiar security is in possession of a written Constitution. Let us not make it a blank paper construction."[13]

What the Constitution forbade, political opportunity invited. In fact, the opportunity was far too good to pass up, and so Jefferson abandoned principle and proceeded with the purchase. The Louisiana Purchase was most certainly the greatest achievement of Jefferson's presidency. Yet the lack of constitutional authorization continued to plague the president. After leaving the presidency, Jefferson received a letter from John B. Colvin, who asked Jefferson if there were times when a president might act outside the law. Jefferson replied: "A strict observance of the written law is doubtless one of the high duties of a good citizen, but it is not *the highest*. The laws of necessity, of self-preservation, of saving our country when in danger, are of higher obligation. To lose our country by a scrupulous adherence to written law, would be to lose the law itself, with life, liberty, property and all those who are enjoying them with us; thus absurdly sacrificing the end to the means."[14] To Jefferson, only "self-preservation," or a great public good, opened the door for a president to act outside the law. And when action is required outside the law, the president must be willing to take a risk, act outside the law, place his actions before the court of public and congressional review, and hope the public and Congress approve such acts. The danger in Jefferson's view is that only *after* the act can judgment be rendered. What if the president acts rashly? Inappropriately? When necessity is not present? Or tragically commits the nation to a foolhardy policy? Jefferson is reduced to an "ends justify the means" argument, but why can the president— alone—decide that the ends truly are worthy of questionable means? And what meaning has the rule of law when even a well-intentioned president may set the law aside to achieve preferred ends?

Jefferson was much pleased with the outcome, writing to General Horatio Gates: "I accept with pleasure, and with pleasure recipro-cate your congratulations on the acquisition of Louisiana; for it is a subject of mutual congratulation, as it is in the interests of every man of the nation. The territory acquired, as it includes all the waters of the Missouri and Mississippi, has more than doubled the area of the United States, and the new part is not inferior to the old in soil, cli-mate, productions, and important communications."[15]

Jefferson remained dubious about his means, and great as the achievement was, it also did constitutional damage. As Jefferson's biographer Merrill Peterson has written, the purchase must be seen as "a revolution in the American Union [that] became a rev-olution in the Constitution. A momentous act of Jeffersonian statesmanship unhinged the Jefferson dogmas and opened so far as precedent might control, the boundless field of power so much feared. Critics then and since found the President inconsistent."[16] In a letter to Abigail Adams, Jefferson wrote that elected officials must "risk themselves like faithful servants . . . and throw them-selves on their country for doing them unauthorized, what we know they would have done for themselves had they been in a sit-uation to do it."[17]

Thomas Jefferson added to the growth of the presidency and to the growth of the nation. He was the first president as party leader, led Congress with skill, used his cabinet effectively, and began to de-velop a more direct link between the president and the people. While articulating a more minimalist view of government than his Federalist predecessors, in office Jefferson fully used, and even ex-panded, the power of the presidency to achieve his goals.

By the time James Monroe assumed the presidency (1817–1825), the tide of power had shifted to Congress, and they jealously guarded their institutional position. The power of congressional committees was on the rise. In this so-called era of good feelings,

Monroe tried to become a nonpartisan chief of state, but Congress wanted no part in it. After Monroe won a second term as president, Speaker Henry Clay concluded, "Mr. Monroe has just been re-elected with apparent unanimity, but he has not the slightest influence on Congress. His career is closed. There was nothing further to be expected by him or from him."[18]

It was in foreign affairs that Monroe is best remembered. Following the collapse of the Spanish empire, several European powers hoped to make political headway in the Americas. In response to fears that France, Russia, or Britain might set up colonies in the hemisphere, Monroe included the following policy pronouncement in his 1823 State of the Union message: "The occasion has been judged proper for asserting, as principle in which the rights and interest of the United States are involved, that the American continents, by the free and independent condition which they have assumed and maintain, are henceforth not to be considered as subjects for future colonization by any European powers." He added:

> We owe, it therefore, to candor and to the amicable relations existing between the United States and those powers to declare that we should consider any attempt on their part to extend their system to any portion of this hemisphere as dangerous to our peace and safety. With the existing colonies or dependencies of any European power we have not interfered and shall not interfere. But with the Governments who have declared their independence and maintained it, and whose independence we have, on great consideration and on just principles, acknowledged, we could not view any interposition for the purpose of oppressing them, or controlling in any other manner their destiny, by any European power in any other light than as the manifestation of an unfriendly deposition toward the United States.

In so announcing, Monroe reinforced a president's independent power to take the initiative and make foreign policy. The Monroe Doctrine was not confirmed by Congress, nor was Monroe required to enforce it during his presidency, but it became one of the pillars of US foreign affairs. In an age of executive weakness, the president could still pull his weight in the making of foreign policy. Despite governing in an era of congressional ascendancy, Monroe did manage to strengthen the power of the presidency in foreign affairs and postponed sectional disputes that were soon to change the era of good feelings to the era of secessionist revolts.

One of the most influential presidents in history, Andrew Jackson (1829–1837), "Old Hickory," was a cantankerous, dueling, iron-willed, ill-tempered street fighter for "the people."[19] John Quincy Adams called him "a barbarian who cannot write a sentence of grammar and can hardly spell his own name." In frail health, in part due to bullets lodged in his body as a result of past duels, Jackson was a dynamic, charismatic figure who "democratized" the presidency and won the support of the people, enhanced the power of the office, and caused no end of trouble for his political adversaries. The first "outsider" to serve as president, Jackson changed both the presidency and the nation.

The Jacksonian era was a turning point in the history of the presidency. Jackson's tenure marked the end of the patrician politics of the founding era. Jackson came to office trumpeting the glory of the common man. "The majority is to govern," he stated in 1829, in his first annual message to Congress. During this period, male suffrage expanded (from 1824 to 1828, the number of males eligible to vote increased from 359,000 to 1,155,400), democratization challenged republican traditions, and the presidency became the tribune of the people, in what carried the potential of becoming a plebiscitary form of national leadership.

Jackson's direct appeals to the people (at that point in history "the people" referred to white males) for political support marked the beginning of efforts to develop what is called an "electoral mandate," an election that empowers a president to lead with the backing of the people. Earlier presidents made no such claims. Elections were not "power-generating events"; they were merely a way to select an officeholder. But Jackson transformed elections into potential mandates. If the president could create the impression that he spoke for and was empowered by "the people," he might have added clout—a mandate—to govern. "The president," Jackson said, "is the direct representative of the American people." Although today such a view seems mundane, in the 1820s it was quite radical. The framers did not want the president to speak for, or even to, "the people." Such a link risked demagoguery. The framers hoped to give the president protection from the will of the people so he could better exercise sound, independent judgment; likewise, they wanted to protect people from the president so that the president could not inflame public passions and impose his will on Congress.

Jackson fundamentally reordered the relationship of the president to the people, laying the groundwork for populist leadership as a way to overcome the roadblocks inherent in the separation of powers. In dismissing the Whig notion that the president was merely to execute the will of Congress, Jackson insisted that it was the president who was the direct representative of the people and as such spoke for the people. Congress should follow the will of the people as expressed through the president. This notion transformed the president from clerk to leader. By "going public," Jackson expanded the presidential arsenal by linking the president to the people. Although few of his immediate successors would fully utilize this opportunity, it nonetheless established a new and potentially significant source of influence for future presidents.

Critics referred to Jackson as "King Andrew" and warned of "executive despotism." Scholar Edward S. Corwin states that the presidency under Jackson was "thrust forward as one of three equal departments of government, and to each and every of its power was imparted new scope, new vitality."[20]

Jackson expanded the spoils system, wherein those who were elected could distribute the spoils (rewards) of government to their political supporters. "To the victor go the spoils" was the order of the day, and Jackson used this system to reward his friends. Jackson expanded the use of the presidential veto to gain power over the legislature and set the national agenda on his terms. Jackson also expanded the president's removal power when, after firing his treasury secretary without approval of Congress, the president established— over the objections of an irate Senate—that a president hires with Senate consent, but fires on his own. The Senate balked, but Jackson maintained they had no business intruding into the business of the executive branch.

The president's ambitious congressional rivals Webster, Clay, and Calhoun postponed their rivalry to join together in efforts to combat the growing power of Jackson. The *New York American* could not believe that "in this land of liberty, *all* the powers of our national government would be usurped by a single man, possessing no one qualification of any single trust, and how, like a maniac, or a driveller, should make it his daily pastime to tear our constitutional charter into rags and tatters, and trample the rights of the people under his feet?" "OUR LIBERTIES ARE IN DANGER," warned the New York Whig convention of 1834. "At this moment, if by your votes you concede the powers that are claimed, your *president* has become your MONARCH."[21]

A key source of Jackson's power was his link to the people. Jackson celebrated the common man. This, of course, greatly threatened the entrenched elites and ran counter to the goals of the framers who sought to insulate the president from popular opinion. "Majority rule, egalitarianism, and power to the people were themes consistently reiterated by President Jackson in his official proclamations and messages to Congress. Pro-Jackson newspapers echoed the president's perspective, while the Democratic party, officially formed by Jackson, served as the president's personal tool for converting democratic rhetoric to public policy."[22] William N. Chambers notes, "At the core of Jackson's importance for the American tradition are four great themes or issues: egalitarianism, democracy, and—as instruments—strong presidential leadership and political party action." Corwin adds, "Jackson was a more dominant party leader than Jefferson."[23]

"Democracy" began to replace "Republicanism" in the American iconography. Now, "the people," not the Constitution, not the representatives of the people, ruled (through the president). This created tensions, and it also elevated the presidency to new heights. The framers harbored fears of mass-based democracy and attempted to insulate the president from the pull of popular passions, while at the same time create a distance between an ambitious president and a potentially powerful ally in the people. The framers feared that the people would animate presidential leadership and that a president might enlist the power of the people in his crusades. Jackson turned the framers' system on its head. Rather than go to the people's representatives, Jackson went directly to the people. He envisioned a presidency in union with the will of the people, serving the majority, not checking it. The president was to be tribune of and for the people. Jackson established a popular base of power from which to lead.

Jackson's battles with Congress reached a peak in a dispute over the recharter of the Bank of the United States. Jackson opposed recharter of what he saw as a bank serving the elites, not the people. Congress voted to recharter the bank against Jackson's objections. He vetoed the legislation. Prior to that time, presidents believed they could veto only legislation they deemed unconstitutional. Jackson transformed the veto power into a policy tool. The president could,

Jackson asserted, veto legislation merely because he disagreed with the contents of a bill on policy grounds. Jackson vetoed more bills (twelve) than all his predecessors combined. This broadening of the veto power opened new doors in presidential bargaining with Congress. From this point on, Congress had to take into consideration the political preferences of the president.[24]

Senator Henry Clay expressed grave concerns over the rise of the populist presidency and the use of popular appeals in the bank dispute:

> Sir, I am surprised and alarmed at the new source of executive power which is found in the result of a presidential election. I had supposed that the Constitution and the laws were the sole source of executive authority . . . that the issue of a presidential election was merely to place the Chief Magistrate in the post assigned to him. But it seems that if, prior to an election certain opinions, no matter how ambiguously put forth by a candidate, are known to the people, those loose opinions, in virtue of the election, incorporate themselves with the Constitution, and afterwards are to be regarded and expounded as parts of the instrument.[25]

Clay sponsored a resolution in the Senate censuring Jackson. It read: "Resolved. That the President, in late Executive proceedings in relation to the public revenue, has assumed upon himself the authority and power not conferred by the Constitution and laws, but in derogation of both." The censure vote, the first of its kind in US history, passed.

During Jackson's presidency issues of slavery and states' rights continued to plague the nation. South Carolina, objecting to a new tariff law, declared the new act of Congress "null, void, and no law, nor binding." Jackson's response to this effort at nullification was swift and firm: "I consider, then, the power to annul a law of the

United States, assumed by one state, incompatible with the existence of the Union, contradicted expressly by the letter of the Constitution, unauthorized by its spirit, inconsistent with every principle on which it was founded, and destructive of the great object for which it was formed." Jackson then sent US troops to the region. Senator Henry Clay came up with a compromise, and the tensions eased, but not before Jackson's vice president, John C. Calhoun, resigned his office to return to South Carolina, run for the Senate, and lead the opposition to Jackson. In the aftermath of this nullification crisis, President Jackson prophetically warned, "The next pretext will be the negro, or slavery question."

Andrew Jackson dramatically changed the presidency. Attaching the presidency to the people created a new and potentially powerful (as well as potentially dangerous) tool of presidential leadership. The framers thought of the House of Representatives as the most democratic branch of government. Jackson saw the presidency as closest to the people. Yet there was an irony in Jackson's new power, well noted by French observer Alexis de Tocqueville: "General Jackson's power is constantly increasing, but that of the president grows less. The federal government is strong in his hands; it will pass to his successor enfeebled."[26]

To be powerful, this new presidency had to be linked to the popular will. Presidential power now rested with the people, as well as the Constitution, and presidents needed to animate popular sentiments, something not easily done. Was the president to *lead* or *follow* the people? Jackson's presidency was "no mere revival of the office; it was a remaking of it."[27]

Referred to as "Young Hickory" because he was a protégé of Andrew Jackson, James Polk (1845–1849) was a strong, assertive president who expanded the office and used war to expand the nation.[28] In his inaugural address, Polk enunciated an expansive view of the presidency:

Although . . . the Chief Magistrate must almost of necessity be chosen by a party and stand pledged to its principles and measures, yet in his official action he should not be the President of a part only, but of the whole people of the United States. While he . . . faithfully carries out in the executive department of the Government the principles and policy of those who have chosen him, he should not be unmindful that our fellow-citizens who have differed with him in opinion are entitled to the full and free exercise of their opinions and judgments, and that the rights of all are entitled to respect and regard.

Like his mentor, Polk saw the presidency as an office of force and leadership. In his first two years in office, his fellow Democrats controlled both houses of Congress, and Polk used this opportunity to chart a bold course in domestic policy, referred to as the "New Democracy." With Polk in the lead, Congress passed tariff reductions and established an independent treasury system. However, it was in foreign affairs that Polk really left his mark.

Polk governed in a time of "Manifest Destiny," a phrase coined by John L. O'Sullivan, editor of the *United States Magazine and Democratic Review*. It reflected the spirit of expansionism. The movement westward was in full swing, and this age recognized few limits. President Polk exploited the nationalist mood and led the nation to significant territorial expansion.

Polk's expansionist agenda sought annexation of Texas and expanding the Oregon border. Getting the Texas territory required some sleight of hand. After being rejected in an effort to purchase the Texas territory from Mexico, President Polk ordered General Zachary Taylor to lead an expedition into Texas. In April 1846, US and Mexican troops clashed, setting off a war in which the United States acquired Texas, New Mexico, and California. By brute force, Polk acquired a tremendously valuable expanse of land. Next to

Jefferson's purchase of the Louisiana Territory, this was the most important land acquisition in US history. Abraham Lincoln, a congressman at the time, spoke of Polk and the Mexican War, calling the president "a bewildered, confounded, and miserably perplexed man." Acquisition of new territory raised thorny issues of sectional balance and slavery. A storm was brewing, and from this point until the Civil War, slavery and sectional rivalries would dominate American politics.

Polk was a powerful, assertive president who expanded the Jacksonian vision of presidential power. Under his leadership, the president began openly to coordinate the development of the federal budget. Although he chose to serve only one term, this was a time of great change and expansion for the nation.

Abraham Lincoln (1861–1865) utterly transformed the presidency as well as the nation. No other president more fully assumed the powers of the office than did Lincoln. He entered the White House when several southern states had already seceded from the Union and civil war seemed an inevitability. "We must not be enemies," said Lincoln, but added that "the Union of these States is perpetual." But it was too late. He couldn't have it both ways.

Lincoln came to power on the eve of the Civil War. His accomplishments—seeing the nation through the Civil War, serving as a war president, freeing the slaves, exercising extraordinary emergency power with grace and skill, preserving the Union, and re-creating the American sense of nationhood—all serve as tribute to his greatness. A nation on the verge of self-destruction was re-created as a fuller, more democratic, and more just country.[29]

As Lincoln prepared for what Emerson called "the hurricane in which he was called to the helm," the new president knew war was inevitable. He did, however, hold out one last olive branch. At the end of his inaugural address he spoke directly to the southern states:

In your hands, my dissatisfied fellow-countrymen, and not in mine, is the momentous issue of civil war. The Government will not assail you. You can have no conflict without being yourselves the aggressors. I am loath to close. We are not enemies but friends. We must not be enemies. Though passion may have strained, it must not break our bonds of affection. The mystic chords of memory, stretching from every battlefield and patriot grave to every living heart and hearthstone all over this broad land, will yet swell the chorus of the Union, when again touched, as surely they will be, by the better angels of our nature.

Events had already eclipsed Lincoln's hopes. There would be war.

The Civil War began during a congressional recess. Lincoln did not, as he might have, call the newly elected Congress into session, nor did he wait for Congress to authorize action—he acted. The president asked, "Must a government of necessity, be too strong for the liberties of its own people, or too weak to maintain its own existence?" Lincoln exercised extraordinary and extraconstitutional power. Lincoln used emergency powers with relative restraint; he used these powers not to subvert democracy but, in his view, to save it. Rejecting normal constitutional limitations, the president believed it was his duty to save the Union. This higher goal justified his emergency actions. In a letter to Salmon Chase, Lincoln wrote, "These rebels are violating the Constitution to destroy the Union; I will violate the Constitution if necessary to save the Union; and I suspect, Chase, that our Constitution is going to have rough time of it before we get done with this row."[30]

To meet the challenge of Civil War, Lincoln took a series of dramatic and constitutionally questionable steps in absence of a declaration of war or congressional authorization: he called up new troops, declared a blockade of southern ports, commenced military action, and suspended habeas corpus. Later, in 1862, he would unilaterally order the emancipation of slaves. This Emancipation Proclamation, which Charles A. Beard calls "the most stupendous act of sequestration in the history of Anglo-Saxon jurisprudence," was ordered without the consent of Congress. Lincoln would defend his actions on the basis of a "doctrine of necessity":

> [My] oath to preserve the Constitution to the best of my ability imposed upon me the duty of preserving, by every indispensable means, that government. . . . Was it possible to lose the nation and yet preserve the Constitution? By general law, life and limb must be protected, yet often a limb must be amputated to save a life; but a life is never wisely given to save a limb. I felt that measures otherwise unconstitutional might become lawful by becoming indispensable to the preservation of the Constitution through the preservation of the nation. Right or wrong, I assumed this ground, and now avow it. I could not feel that, to the best of my ability, I had even tried to preserve the Constitution, if, to save slavery or any minor matter I should permit the wreck of government, country, and Constitution all together.[31]

The Civil War forced Lincoln to change the very relationship of the presidency to the constitutional order. The unprecedented emergency of the Civil War, Lincoln believed, allowed him to assume power no previous president claimed. He would not allow the Union to dissolve and the nation to crumble. The president had taken an oath to preserve the union and make sure the laws were faithfully executed. The southern rebellion was preventing that. Thus, Lincoln asked, "Are all of the laws *but one* to go unexecuted, and the Government itself go to pieces lest that one be violated?"[32]

Some critics charged Lincoln with setting up a dictatorship. Lincoln felt he had no other choice. Lincoln's use of prerogative power during the Civil War was daunting.[33] So broadly did Lincoln interpret his emergency power that some scholars describe it as a "constitutional dictatorship."[34] Lincoln admitted that some of his actions were not "strictly legal," yet they were necessary. Thus, Lincoln greatly expanded the scope of emergency presidential power.

As the war proceeded slowly and painfully toward Union victory, Lincoln used the opportunity to redefine American nationhood. He did so in a variety of ways, but nowhere is his vision more clearly articulated than in his Gettysburg and second inaugural addresses.

On the battlefield of Gettysburg, Lincoln sanctified the sacrifice made by the troops who died, but he also distilled the true meaning of the war in very few words. The blood of the dead and the sacred honor of the past merged to create "a new birth of freedom." The address fused the sacred with the secular, with images of sacrifice and redemption. Those brave men died for an abstract but powerful idea: "the proposition that all men are created equal" and that "government of the people, by the people, for the people, shall not perish from the earth." In a mere 272 words, Lincoln transformed the purpose of the nation. The address, printed in its entirety, reads:

> Four score and seven years ago our fathers brought forth on this continent, a new nation, conceived in Liberty, and dedicated to the proposition that all men are created equal.
>
> Now we are engaged in a great civil war, testing whether that nation or any nation so conceived and so dedicated, can long endure. We are met on a great battle-field of that war. We have come to dedicate a portion of that field, as a final resting place for those who here gave their lives that that nation might live. It is altogether fitting and proper that we should do this.
>
> But, in a larger sense, we can not dedicate—we can not consecrate—we can not hallow—this ground. The brave men, living and dead, who struggled here, have consecrated it, far above our poor power to add or detract. The world will little note, nor long

remember what we say here, but it can never forget what they did here. It is for us the living, rather, to be dedicated here to the unfinished work which they who fought here have thus far so nobly advanced. It is rather for us to be here dedicated to the great task remaining before us—that from these honored dead we take increased devotion to that cause for which they gave the last full measure of devotion—that we here highly resolve that these dead shall not have died in vain—that this nation, under God, shall have a new birth of freedom—and that government of the people, by the people, for the people, shall not perish from the earth.

Lincoln gave meaning to the events of the Civil War by linking the past (the founding and the Declaration of Independence) with the present (tragedy of war, loss, and sacrifice) and the future (the survivors were to create "a new birth of freedom"). It was a shift from negative liberty to positive liberty, a dramatic transformation of the American ethos. Lincoln elevated the Declaration of Independence over the Constitution as a primary American icon. As historian Garry Wills notes, "Lincoln not only put the Declaration in a new light as a matter of founding *law*, but put its central proposition, equality, in a newly favored position as a principle of the Constitution."[35]

In Lincoln's second inaugural address he revisited many of the themes presented at Gettysburg, but his tone was more somber and religious. The war was divine punishment for the sin of slavery:

The Almighty has His own purposes. "Woe unto the world because of offences! For it must needs be that offences come; but woe to that man by whom the offence cometh!" If we shall suppose that American Slavery is one of the offences which, in the providence of God, must needs come, but which, having continued through His appointed time, He now will to remove, and that

He gives to both North and South, this terrible war, as the woe due to those by whom the offence came, shall we discern therein any departure from those divine attributes which the believers in a Living God always ascribe to Him? Fondly do we hope—fervently do we pray—that this might scourge of war may speedily pass away. Yet, if God will that it continue, until all the wealth piled by the bond-man's two hundred and fifty years of requited toil shall be sunk, and until every drop of blood drawn with the lash, shall be paid by another drawn with the sword, as was said three thousand years ago, so still it must be said "the judgments of the Lord, are true and righteous altogether."

With malice toward none; with charity for all; with firmness in the right, as God gives us to see the right, let us strive on to finish the work we are in; to bind up the nation's wound; to care for him who shall have borne the battle, and for his widow, and his orphan—to do all which may achieve and cherish a just, and a lasting peace, among ourselves, and with all nations.

As political scientist Bruce Miroff has written:

With the war all but won, with his reelection secured and his place in history already taking form, Lincoln was ready to ask more of the American people than he had ever done before. The second inaugural address called for a painful self-examination, so that the American people could come to terms with their historic failings. Lincoln himself had undergone this self-examination and had accepted the "humiliation" it necessitated. Remaining close to the people as a democratic leader, he asked them to share his experience and to face the deepest truths about themselves. The democratic leader would not speak to the people from on high or proclaim the superiority of his own political burdens; he would educate the people about a legacy of guilt and a possibility of redemption that leader and followers shared. In the second inaugural address, Lincoln left a remarkable example of what democratic leadership in American might attempt to be.[36]

The cumulative effect of these two dramatic speeches underscored the shift that was taking place in the United States. As historian James McPherson has written: "The United States went to war in 1861 to preserve the *Union*; it emerged from war in 1865 having created a *nation*. Before 1861 the two words 'United States' were generally used as a plural noun: the 'United States are a republic.' After 1865 the United States became a singular noun. The loose union of states became a nation. Lincoln's wartime speeches marked this transition."[37]

While Lincoln was a masterful politician, during most of his presidency he was largely unpopular and often unsuccessful at meeting his war aims, getting Congress to bend to his will, or even at times controlling his own administration. During the Civil War, Lincoln dominated the American government. Careful to relate his actions to his "duty as commander-in-chief," Lincoln engaged in actions that were clearly unconstitutional. But Lincoln held out the possibility that his authority stemmed from the Constitution itself, stating, "As commander-in-chief of the Army and Navy in time of war, I suppose I have a right to take any measure which may best subdue the enemy."[38]

Lincoln seemed to claim a right to act in disregard of or against the Constitution when a national emergency threatened the government. When Congress was unavailable, so Lincoln's reasoning went, the president had the right—even the duty—to act, even if his actions were in direct violation of the law. Lincoln also suggested that he was justified in his actions because the president possessed certain war powers that allowed him to act in defense of the Union. Since the oath of office he took called upon him to "preserve, protect, and defend the Constitution," Lincoln's actions were—in his eyes at least—taken to uphold that oath. His efforts were, he suggested, to preserve the Constitution, and thus were justified (if not strictly legal).

Lincoln's violations of personal rights and liberty were significant. After the outbreak of hostilities, the president decided that the procedures for controlling disloyalty were inadequate. He decided that the right to habeas corpus should be suspended and that civilians should be tried in military courts. Three court cases are of particular interest to us regarding this issue.

Ex Parte Merryman (17 Fed. Cas. 144, No. 9487, 1861): One of the victims of Lincoln's orders was John Merryman. Mr. Merryman was a civilian being held under military arrest without privilege of habeas corpus (he was accused of treason). He petitioned Chief Justice Taney of the Supreme Court for a writ of habeas corpus. Taney, acting alone, defied Lincoln and ordered that the writ be issued. In that decision, Taney suggested that the president had no power to suspend habeas corpus, that the military had no power to detain a civilian (even if ordered by the president), and that Merryman was entitled to immediate release. The commanding general in this matter, George Cadwalader, refused to honor the chief justice's order on the grounds that he was authorized by the president to suspend the writ. Taney was helpless; all he could do was file his opinion and write, "I have exercised all the power which the constitution and laws confer upon me, but that power has been resisted by a force too strong for me to overcome."[39] As Clinton Rossiter has written regarding this case: "The one great precedent is what Lincoln did, not what Taney said. Future Presidents will know where to look for historical support. So long as public opinion sustains the President, as a sufficient amount of it sustained Lincoln in his shadowy tilt with Taney and throughout the rest of the war, he has nothing to fear from the displeasure of the courts."[40]

Ex Parte Milligan (4 Wallace 2, 18 L. Ed. 281, 1866): L. P. Milligan, along with some associates, was arrested in Indiana by the military and accused of treason. He was sentenced to be hanged, but President Johnson commuted the sentence to life imprisonment. Milligan petitioned the courts, which unanimously held that the military commission was unlawful and that Milligan was to be freed.

On the surface it appears that the Court acted boldly and stood up to the president in its defense of the rights of Mr. Milligan, but did it? When the Court handed down its decision, the war was over, the danger subsided, and Lincoln, the initiator of Milligan's internment, was dead and buried. The Court's decision did not affect the president who ordered the action, and it did not affect the emergency faced by the Union.

The words of the Court in its defense of the rights of Mr. Milligan are grand, but the words do not reflect the realities of the political conflict that developed between the president and the courts, a conflict the courts conveniently avoided until Lincoln had long since left the scene. The words of Justice Davis, while inspiring, seem a bit absurd when one considers the context in which they were delivered. Davis's statement read, in part: "The constitution of the United States is a law for rulers and people, equally in war and peace, and covers with the shield of its protection all classes of men, at all times, and under all circumstances. No doctrine, involving more pernicious consequences was ever invented by the writ of man than that any of its provisions can be suspended during any of the great exigencies of government."[41] And of this, Clinton Rossiter writes:

> As a restraint upon a President beset by martial crisis it was then, and is now, of practically no value whatsoever. It cannot be emphasized too strongly that the decision in this case followed the close of the rebellion by a full year, altered not in the slightest de-

gree the extraordinary methods through which that rebellion had been suppressed, and did nothing more than deliver from jail a handful of rascals who in any event would have probably gained their freedom in short order. . . . In sum, *Ex Parte Milligan* is sound doctrine forbidding the presidential establishment of military commissions for the trial of civilians in areas where the civil courts are open—but it is little else. Its general observations on the war powers are no more valid today than they were in 1866 [*sic*]. Here again the law of the Constitution is what Lincoln did in the crisis, not what the court said later.[42]

Prize Cases, 67 US 2 Black 635 (1863): The Prize Cases rose out of the president's blockade of the confederacy, which Lincoln ordered in the early days of the Civil War. Four ships had been captured by Union forces and brought into ports and labeled as "prizes." The Supreme Court was called upon once to decide a question of presidential power. The Court was asked whether the president, in a time of war, had the right to order this blockade. The Court, in a 5–4 decision, answered yes. Justice Grier wrote:

> If a war be made by invasion of a foreign nation, the President is not only authorized to resist by force. He does not initiate the war, but is bound to accept the challenges without waiting for any special legislative authority. And whether the hostile party be foreign invader, or States organized in rebellion, it is nonetheless a war, although the declaration of it be "*unilateral. . . .*"
>
> This greatest of civil wars was not gradually developed by popular commotion, tumultuous assemblies, or local unorganized insurrections. However long may have been its previous conception, it nevertheless sprung forth suddenly from the parent brain, a Minerva in the full panoply of *war*. The President was bound to meet it in the shape it presented itself, without waiting for

Congress to baptize it with a name; and no name given to it by him or them could change the fact. . . .

Whether the President is fulfilling his duties as Commander-in-chief, in suppressing an insurrection, has met with such armed hostile resistance, and a civil war of such alarming proportions will compel him according to them the character of belligerents, is a question to be decided by him, and this Court must be governed by the decision and acts of the political department of the Government to which this power was entrusted. He must determine what degree of force the crisis demands. The proclamation of blockade is itself official and conclusive evidence to the Court that a state of war existed which demanded and authorized a recourse to such a measure, under the circumstance peculiar to the case.[43]

The Prize Cases serve as yet another example of a court rationalizing presidential extensions of power in emergencies.[44] The president, acting without a congressionally declared war and in the absence of authorizing legislation, ordered the blockade. The courts agreed with this extension of presidential power. In the future this case would have an important bearing on presidents who sought to expand the boundaries of their power.

If, as Justice Grier wrote, the question of how hostilities will be met must be decided "by him" (the president), then who is to stand up and defend the rights of the citizenry, the Constitution, and statutes? Justice Grier's view sounds dangerously similar to Locke's "prerogative" power. If the president decides all matters of policy relating to wars and hostilities, there are no safeguards. Here the importance of the Court diminishes in the face of the emergency powers of the president.

President Lincoln's actions during the Civil War, his repeated extensions of presidential power, his extraconstitutional actions led him to the position, critics charged, of quasi-dictator. The Supreme

Court (Justice Taney, sitting as circuit justice), when asked to review the president's actions, responded by making a weak attempt to check the president in the *Merryman* case, backing away from the president until the crisis and the president had passed away in the *Milligan* case, and backing away from the already bloated powers of the president in the *Prize Cases*. The Court's record is not an altogether distinguished one when we look at the realities of the cases instead of the words that the Court chose to condemn Lincoln.

The Court's intent in *Merryman* may have been genuine and well founded, but it did not attempt to do more than have the chief justice make a lame appeal to the president. This was an excellent example of just how weak the courts can be when facing a resolute president. In the *Milligan* case, the Court's words were strong and well presented, but they were too late. The Court in the Civil War did little to control presidential extensions of power. Perhaps there was little it could have done.

Additional examples of Lincoln's emergency actions include the seizure of newspapers, arrest of editors,[45] and the famous Emancipation Proclamation—issued under his powers as commander-in-chief in time of war. During the Civil War (and perhaps because of it), Lincoln acted either in the absence of congressional consent or in disregard of it.[46]

When faced with the domestic crisis of the Civil War, Lincoln became a "constitutional dictator." He assumed "prerogative" power and took unto himself powers otherwise reserved for the other branches of government. The Civil War presidency of Abraham Lincoln serves as an example of the differences in power between the "normal conditions presidency" (limited) and the "emergency presidency" (powerful).

4

The Presidency Takes
Center Stage, 1866–2000

Throughout American history, one can see a recurring pattern wherein a strong, assertive president acts boldly, adds tools to the presidential power arsenal, and enlarges the office and its powers, and then a series of weak presidents follow. This action-reaction cycle leads to dramatic swings in presidential power. After a strong executive, Congress, seeing its institutional power sapped, reasserts itself, and a period of presidency-bashing occurs. This roller-coaster ride still adds to the president's potential powers in the long run, but the seesaw nature of action-reaction tames—for a time at least—the growth of presidential power.

After Jackson, lesser flames such as Van Buren, Harrison, and Tyler presided but did not govern. After Polk came the weaker presidencies of Taylor, Fillmore, Pierce, and Buchanan. This pattern vividly occurred in the aftermath of Abraham Lincoln's powerful presidency. After Lincoln, Congress reclaimed some of its powers and held the presidents in check. For forty years, presidents seemed weak and ineffectual. The series of very forgettable presidents—Hayes, Garfield, Arthur, Cleveland, Harrison—often played second fiddle to a more powerful Congress.

In this era of weak presidents, the observant Englishman James Bryce wrote an influential two-volume history of politics in the United States titled *The American Commonwealth* (1888). Bryce remarked on the many changes that had taken place in America, from territorial expansion to economic growth, all of which called for a more powerful central government.[1] Bryce famously titled one of his chapters "Why Great Men Are Not Chosen President." Bryce compared American presidents to British prime ministers and found the American executives wanting. He saw the British parliamentary system, which allows for a strong executive, as superior to America's brand of congressional government. Congress dominated, and therefore great men did not seek the presidency because the office itself was too weak.[2]

President William McKinley (1897–1901) was something of a presidential paradox. Frequently portrayed as weak, he nonetheless (albeit reluctantly) exerted significant presidential and US power on the world stage. In some ways he displayed a regressive brand of conservatism, promoting high tariffs and embracing jingoistic imperialism abroad. He also led the nation into the global arena, declaring, "Isolation is no longer possible or desirable." McKinley expanded presidential power and began the nation's venture into empire and imperial conquest. He helped transform the role of president from national clerk to global leader.

In truth, McKinley may have been more swept up by events than in control of them. It was a time of growth and change. Henry Jones Ford, whom scholar Edward S. Corwin calls "the real herald of the twentieth-century presidency," wrote the influential book *The Rise and Growth of American Politics*, in 1898. Ford accurately predicted the rise of presidential power: "It is the product of political conditions which dominate all departments of government, so that Congress itself shows an unconscious disposition to aggrandize the presidential office. . . . The truth is that in the presidential office, as it has been constituted since Jackson's time, American democracy has revived the oldest political institution of the race, the elective kingship. It is all there: the precognition of the notables and the tumultuous choice of the freemen, only conformed to modern conditions."[3] A passive president seemed no longer possible for the growing republic. Events demanded bolder, more assertive, and centralized leadership. As America became a global power, it also became a presidential nation. Thus, some historians refer to William McKinley as the first modern president.

The Spanish-American War, in 1898, was a major transforming event in the life of the nation. The war itself, sometimes referred to as "the splendid little war," lasted but a few months; however, its impact was revolutionary. After the US victory, Spain lost nearly all its colonial interests in the Americas, and the United States became a recognized world power—an imperial or colonial power that occupied nations outside its borders. The United States now controlled Cuba, the Philippines, and Puerto Rico as a result of the Paris Peace Treaty in December 1898.

During the McKinley presidency, a significant shift in political power occurred. Congress declined and the executive rose. Our understanding of the Constitution's meaning changed as well, as McKinley, along with Teddy Roosevelt and Woodrow Wilson, would expand presidential power to fill America's new global role. In the area of foreign affairs, McKinley enhanced presidential authority. He conducted a presidential war, largely on his own claimed authority, and acquired the Philippines (using an executive order and bypassing the Senate); his secretary of state, John Hay, established an open-door policy for China; and in 1900, without congressional approval, McKinley dispatched five thousand troops to China to suppress the Boxer Rebellion. By waging war, acting unilaterally, bypassing Congress, establishing an empire, and doing this "solely" on executive authority, McKinley shifted the balance of power (especially in foreign affairs) in favor of the presidency.

Then, tragedy struck. In September 1901, McKinley traveled to Buffalo, New York, to open the Pan-American Exposition. As he greeted visitors, he noticed a man approach him whose hand was wrapped in a bandage. As McKinley reached out to shake the man's other hand, two shots rang out from a pistol concealed beneath the bandages. A week later, the president was dead. "Good Lord," exclaimed Senator Mark Hanna, "that Goddamn cowboy is President of the United States."

"It is," President Theodore Roosevelt (1901–1909) (TR) wrote to a friend, "a dreadful thing to come into the Presidency this way; but it would be a far worse thing to be morbid about it. Here is the task, and I have got to do it to the best of my ability; and that is all there is about it."[4]

With a puffy face, droopy mustache, thick-lensed pince-nez eyeglasses, prominent teeth, and a high voice, Theodore Roosevelt helped transform the presidency and convert the office into a truly national leadership institution. It was in the Roosevelt era that the presidency first began to resemble the institution with which we are familiar today.

TR was an activist president who by the sheer force of will stamped his personality onto his age. Roosevelt exerted policy leadership as a "conservative-progressive" à la Disraeli, the British prime minister who saw himself as a conservative who advocated progressive public policy reforms. He transformed the presidency into a more public office, using (some would say abusing) the "bully pulpit" to elevate the rhetorical presidency to new heights and developing a more sophisticated relationship between the president and the press.

At the turn of the century, the presidency was a mere suggestion of what it would eventually become. McKinley did not fully exploit the opportunity to gain power afforded by the rise of the United States as a world power.[5] TR would not let the opportunity slip through his hands. He loved power, relished in its exercise, and utterly sought to dominate. The result, he later boasted, was that "I did and caused to be done many things not previously done by the President and the heads of the departments. I did not usurp power, but I did greatly broaden the use of executive power. In other words, I acted for the public welfare, I acted for the common well-being of all our people, whenever and in whatever manner was necessary, unless prevented by direct constitutional or legislative prohibition." Under TR, the presidency became the center of the American political universe. His gravitational pull, his flair for self-dramatization, the utter strength of his personality allowed a powerful president to direct the government and set the political agenda.

Historian Louis Hartz calls Roosevelt "America's only Nietzschean president." A contemporary of Roosevelt's said, "At every wedding, Theodore wants to be the bride. At every funeral he wants to be the corpse." "He is," said Henry James, "the very embodiment of noise." And muckraker Ida Tarbell wrote this of TR: "I felt his clothes might not contain him, he was so steamed up, so ready to go, to attack anything, anywhere." Roosevelt's need to lead every parade compelled him to exert himself, even force himself, onto center stage. He courted public opinion; he was the president as "national celebrity." Did any other president delight in the exercise of powers more than Teddy Roosevelt? But conditions, as he recognized, were not ripe for greatness. "If there is not the great occasion," he noted, "you don't get *the* great statesman; if Lincoln had lived in times of peace no one would have known his name now." In 1897 he wrote, "If this country could be ruled by a benevolent czar, we would doubtless make a good many changes for the better."

TR had an obsession with masculinity that bordered on the pathological.[6] As Bruce Miroff writes, "He portrayed a world divided between the timid men of words, sitting in the stands and carping at their betters, and the heroic men of action, gladiators in the political arena." In a 1910 speech at the Sorbonne in Paris,

Roosevelt said, "It is not the critic who counts; not the man who points out how the strong man stumbles, or where the doer of deeds could have done them better. The credit belongs to the man who is actually in the arena, whose face is marred by dust and sweat and blood; who strives valiantly; who errs, and comes short again and again, because there is no effort without error or shortcoming; but who does actually strive to do the deeds." He "reserved his greatest contempt for 'emasculated sentimentalists.'" TR believed in the strenuous life. He once said of his sons, "I would rather one of them should die, than have them grow up weaklings." In Roosevelt, masculinity merged with moral righteousness to form "an ego of heroic proportions."[7]

TR was among a handful of presidents who substantially increased the authority and responsibility of the office. He may have built on the foundation of predecessors, but few presidents did as much as TR to fundamentally alter the presidency. He changed the office, whereas others merely held it. He led where others presided.

Roosevelt had an expansionist view of presidential power. He *personalized* the office, linking policy to personality. In his first annual message to Congress, TR summed up his view of how American society had changed and how the role of government needed to change as well: "When the Constitution was adopted, at the end of the eighteenth century, no human wisdom could foretell the sweeping changes, alike in industrial and political conditions, which were to take place at the beginning of the twentieth century. At that time it was accepted as a matter of course that the several States were the proper authorities to regulate so far as was then necessary, the comparatively insignificant and strictly localized corporate bodies of the day. The conditions are now wholly different and wholly different action is called for."

If the president was to serve as the "steward of the people," he was also to be the centerpiece of political action. Roosevelt not only changed the way the presidency was viewed but also changed the way it operated, establishing a very close and personal relationship between the president and the public. This connection may have had its roots with Andrew Jackson, but it came into full bloom under TR. He helped turn the executive into a personal office and a people's presidency, using the "bully pulpit" to reach out to the public. Here, the rhetorical presidency was truly born. And TR scoffed at his critics:

> While President, I have *been* President, emphatically; I have used every ounce of power there was in the office and I have not cared a rap for the criticisms of those who spoke of my "usurpation of power"; for I knew that the talk was all nonsense and that there was no usurpation. I believe that the efficiency of this Government depends upon its possessing a strong central executive, and wherever I could establish a precedent of strength in the executive . . . I have felt not merely that my action was right in itself, but that I was establishing a precedent of value.[8]

TR extended executive authority further than any other peacetime president. Plus, his linking of the president to the public established a new theory of government built on a Jacksonian foundation. The president, to Roosevelt, was the chief spokesman for the people.

Roosevelt was a whirlwind of a man who sought to utterly dominate people and events. He asserted a claim that the president should be the nation's chief legislator and pushed himself deeper into the legislative arena than any of his predecessors. TR outlined his proposals in public speeches and messages to Congress. He even went so far as to draft bills and send them to Congress. In the past, this was done quietly behind the scenes, for fear that presidents might be accused of overstepping their separation-of-power bounds. TR also worked hard lobbying Congress on behalf of his legislative proposals. "A good executive," he asserted, "under the present conditions of American political life, must take a very active interest in getting the right kind of legislation." (He once lamented, "Oh, if I could only be President and Congress together for just ten minutes!") Roosevelt's ambitious legislative agenda, referred to as the Square Deal, included antitrust legislation, the Hepburn Act, conservation, the creation of the Department of Commerce and Labor, and a variety of other progressive policy proposals.

If TR was innovative in the domestic arena, he was even more activist and controversial in foreign affairs. Whereas McKinley introduced America to the world stage, it was Roosevelt who determined to dominate it. He talked of speaking softly but carrying a big stick, increased the size of the US Navy, imposed a deal that led to the building of the Panama Canal, and brokered a peace agreement, ending the Russo-Japanese War (for which he was the first American president to receive a Nobel Peace Prize). When the Senate refused to ratify a treaty with the Dominican Republic, Roosevelt merely ignored the will of the Senate and signed it as an Executive Agreement. Roosevelt defended this decision, arguing, "The Constitution did not explicitly give me power to bring about the necessary agreement with Santo Domingo. . . . But, the Constitution did not forbid my doing what I did. I put the agreement into effect, and I continued its execution for two years before the Senate acted; and I would have continued it until the end of my term if necessary, without any action by Congress."[9] Mr. Roosevelt was no wallflower.

Roosevelt also added a critical tool to the president's power arsenal when he intervened militarily in Santo Domingo. Done ostensibly to protect the interests of US companies doing business there, Roosevelt defended his decision on grounds that the United States had a right to establish and guarantee hemispheric order. The United States was the sheriff of the hemisphere. "It is our duty," he said, "when it becomes absolutely inevitable to police these countries in the interest of order and civilization." This act—the Roosevelt corollary to the Monroe Doctrine—added yet another weapon to the president's already enlarging arsenal. In a speech directed at the United States' Latin American neighbors, Roosevelt said:

> It is not true that the United States feels any land hunger or entertains any projects as regards the other nations of the western hemisphere save such as for their welfare. All that this country desires is to see the neighboring countries stable, orderly and prosperous . . . if a nation shows that it knows how to act with reasonable efficiency and decency in social and political matters, if it keeps order and pays its obligations, it need fear no interference by the United States. Chronic wrongdoing, or an impotence which results in a general loosening of the ties of civilized society may in America, as elsewhere, ultimately require intervention by some civilized nation, and in the western hemisphere the adherence of the United States to the Monroe Doctrine may force the United States, however reluctantly, in flagrant cases of such wrongdoing or impotence, to the exercise of an international police power.

Teddy Roosevelt changed the Constitution—not the wording, but the interpretation and understanding of the scope and nature of executive power. He stretched the constitutional limits further than any president since Lincoln, and in doing so, he helped invent a "new" institution, and redefined the presidency.

TR was a dynamo, a bundle of energy, a man of action. He left the presidency bigger than when he arrived. Future presidents could lay claim to roles of chief legislator, tribune of and spokesman for the people, world leader, steward of the people, and national leader.

Not all his successors did, but TR paved the way for those who embraced an expansive view of presidential power to stamp their identity onto the political scene.

This was a time when the Hamilton-Jefferson debate over the scope of presidential power was presented anew. This time, however, there were dueling presidents, with Theodore Roosevelt pitted against his handpicked successor, William Howard Taft.

The Progressive movement had significant impact on the politics of this age, and Progressives, reacting to the rapid changes going on in American society such as industrialization, urbanization, and the rise of the United States in power abroad, saw the Constitution as outdated and in need of modernization. Progressives placed their hopes in a more powerful presidency to overcome the slow, parochial nature of Congress.

The Progressive Teddy Roosevelt offered an expansionist view of presidential power. This Hamiltonian interpretation called for the president to boldly lead the nation, as TR saw presidential power as expansive, not narrow. He wrote of what came to be called the stewardship theory of presidential power:

The executive power was limited only by specific restrictions and prohibitions appearing in the Constitution or imposed by the Congress under its Constitutional powers. My view was that every executive office, and above all every executive office in high position, was a steward of the people bound actively and affirmatively to do all he could for the people. . . . I declined to adopt the view that what was imperatively necessary for the Nation could not be done by the President unless he could find some specific authorization to do it. My belief was that it was not only his right but his duty to do anything that the needs of the Nation demanded unless such action was forbidden by the Constitution or by the laws.[10]

He continued: "Under this interpretation of executive power I did and caused many thing not previously done by the president and the heads of the departments. I did not usurp power, but I greatly broadened the use of executive power. In other words, I acted for the public welfare, I acted for the common well-being of all our people, whenever and in whatever manner was necessary, unless prevented by direct constitutional or legislative prohibition."[11]

William Howard Taft maintained a more circumscribed view of presidential power. Writing after he left the presidency, yet before TR's autobiography was published, Taft took a more legalistic and restrained view of the president's powers. To Taft, the president was authorized to act *only* on the basis of a constitutionally granted power.[12] This was also the stance initially taken by Taft's successor, Woodrow Wilson.

Before becoming president, Wilson was a political science professor, noted author, and, later, president of Princeton University. Much of Wilson's academic writing focuses on the relationship between Congress and the president. In his first major work *Congressional Government* (1885), he argued that the framers created congressional government, with a limited executive.[13] In his next major work, *Constitutional Government in the United States* (1908), however, Wilson changed his tune. Here, Wilson saw parliamentary reform as the way to rescue American government from the legislative vortex. Strong party government, he argued, would allow a strong Congress to be guided by a strong president. As Wilson wrote:

Our life has undergone radical changes since 1787, and almost every change has operated to draw the nation together, to give it the common consciousness, the common interests, the common standards of conduct, the habit of concerted action which will eventually impart to it many more aspects of the character of a single community. . . .

It is difficult to describe any single part of a great governmental system without describing the whole of it. Governments are living things and operate as organic wholes. Moreover, governments have their natural evolution and are one thing in one age, another in another. The makers of the Constitution constructed the federal government upon a theory of checks and balances which was meant to limit the operation of each part and allow to no single part or organ of it a dominating force; but no government can be successfully conducted upon so mechanical a theory.

Wilson saw the president as the focal point for this system. He believed that over the span of American history, the people had grown to see the president as the key that ties together the US government as the leader "both of his party and the nation." Thus, for Wilson, "The President is at liberty, both in law and conscience, to be as big a man as he can. His capacity will set the limit; and if Congress be overborne by him, it will be no fault of the makers of the Constitution,—it will be no lack of constitutional powers on its part, but only because the President has the nation behind him, and Congress has not. He has no means of compelling Congress except through public opinion."[14]

Wilson used party and popular leadership to move Congress.[15] He was also a wartime president who exerted extraconstitutional leadership, not only in the war, but also in the aftermath of war to promote an expansive and idealistic peace. In a way there were three different Wilson presidencies: the highly successful domestic reformer of the first term, the successful war president during World War I, and the idealistic, but in the end tragic, crusader for world peace toward the end of his presidency.

Wilson broke a Jeffersonian precedent by personally addressing a special session of Congress—the first time this occurred since the presidency of John Adams. This marked the beginning of an annual tradition, where the president personally delivers the State of the Union address to Congress. In 1913, shortly after his inauguration, Wilson held the first presidential press conference. Soon, the press conference became institutionalized. Wilson used these press conferences to promote both himself and his reform policies.

President Wilson aggressively pursued his legislative agenda in Congress. In his first term, he used party and popular leadership as a source of pressure to achieve a number of domestic reforms, known as the New Freedom. Legislation to break monopolies, assist unions, and lower tariffs was passed. Child labor laws, a newly created Federal Reserve, and a series of other laws were passed as well. Wilson noted, "It is only once in a generation that a people can be lifted above material things. That is why conservative government is in the saddle two-thirds of the time." Thus, as president he pushed hard to achieve as much as possible. But there was also a dark side to his leadership. Wilson's attitude about race relations led him to further impose segregation in several government departments, and his administration carried out significant internal repression during World War I.

The Wilson administration also incurred a Supreme Court test of the president's removal power in *Myers v. United States*.[16] Frank S. Myers was named a first-class postmaster by President Woodrow Wilson in 1917. In 1920, Wilson asked for Myers's resignation, but Myers refused. Myers was removed from office by order of the postmaster general, acting under the direction of Wilson. Myers protested, citing the act of Congress of July 12, 1876, that said removal of a first-class postmaster could be effective only if the president acted with the consent of Congress. Wilson neither requested nor received such consent.

The Supreme Court, with Chief Justice Taft writing the majority opinion, denied Myers's claim (brought by his heirs) and ruled in favor of the president's removal. Taft based his decision on the premise that this point was thoroughly argued by the First Congress (many of whom participated in the Constitutional Convention), and they had decided that the president did have removal power. Taft argued: "The ordinary duties officers prescribed by statute come under the general administrative control of the President by virtue of the general grant to him of the executive power, and he may properly supervise and guide their construction of the statutes under which they act in order to secure that unitary and uniform execution of the laws which Article II of the Constitution evidently contemplated in vesting general executive power in the President alone. Finding such officers to be negligent and inefficient, the President should have the power to remove them."

President Wilson's great success as a reformer during his first term led to reelection, as during the campaign Wilson promised to keep the United States out of war in Europe. But this was a promise he was unable to keep, and Wilson soon became a war president. During World War I, Wilson demonstrated skill and determination. On January 8, 1918, he delivered his "Fourteen Points" speech to Congress, a comprehensive postwar plan for peace, calling for greater justice for small nations, self-determination for "enslaved" nations, and arbitration of international dispute.

After the war, Wilson went to work building what he referred to as a "lasting peace." He went to Europe to negotiate not only a settlement to the war, but a plan for the postwar peace as well. The result was the Treaty of Versailles, which Wilson brought back to the United States for Senate approval. (He won a Nobel Peace Prize for his efforts.) The Senate, now controlled by Republicans, balked at the proposal, rejecting Wilson's plan and also the League of Nations the president was proposing.

Wilson took this snub personally and took his case directly to the people. World War I was supposed to "make the world safe for democracy," and Wilson was not about to let the Senate interfere with his plans for a League of Nations and postwar peace. But Wilson was too rigid to compromise. He wanted it all and would settle for nothing less. This intransigence with Senate Republicans doomed the treaty. As matters went from bad to worse, Wilson became more and more rigid. He took an exhausting national tour on behalf of "his" treaty. Soon fatigue and illness overtook him. Finally, he suffered a stroke that left him bedridden.

During his incapacitation, his wife, Edith Wilson, all but ran the country, leading critics to sneer, "We have a petticoat government." The physically weakened Wilson remained uncompromising about the League of Nations. His all-or-nothing attitude eventually led to nothing. Wilson's presidency ended with a debilitated and disappointed president, unable to achieve his final and biggest victory.

After the activism of Teddy Roosevelt and Woodrow Wilson, the swelling of the presidency gave way to an era of small presidents: Coolidge, Harding, and Hoover. But events that would again lead to demands for greater presidential activism inevitably occurred.

The Creation of the Modern Presidency

Usually considered one of the three greatest presidents in history, Franklin D. Roosevelt (1933–1945) (FDR) brought the nation through two crises: an economic depression and a world war and transformed the nation and the presidency in the process.

Roosevelt is often credited with creating the "modern presidency." He transformed the presidency from a rather small, personalized office into a massive institution. (In 1931, there were approximately 600,000 federal employees; by 1941, that number topped 1.4 million.) Facing the crises of the Depression and World War II, FDR contributed to the creation of both the welfare state and the warfare state. When he died early in his fourth term, Roosevelt left America a vastly different nation than when he first took office in 1933.

FDR became the model of the modern president. All successors have been compared (unfavorably) to him. He cast, as historian William Luchtenberg notes, "a giant shadow."

Roosevelt needed to get off to a fast start. Roughly 15 million Americans were unemployed, forty-six hundred banks failed, and industrial production fell below 50 percent of the 1929 level. His inaugural address called the nation to noble enterprise to meet the challenge of depression: "It is hoped that the normal balance of executive and legislative authority may be wholly adequate to meet the unprecedented task before us. . . . But in the event that . . . the national emergency is still critical . . . I shall ask the Congress for one remaining instrument to meet the crisis—broad executive power to wage a war against the emergency, as great as the power that would be given to me if we were in fact invaded by a foreign foe."

On his first day in office Roosevelt declared a "bank holiday," and four days later he proposed the Emergency Banking Bill. It was the beginning of one of the most extraordinary times in American politics: "the hundred days." From March 9 to June 15, an unrelenting succession of bills was passed by Congress.

Creatively using the technology available to him, FDR took his case directly to the people in the form of "fireside chats," radio addresses in which the president forged a close and direct link to the American people. Not only were the addresses informative and reassuring, but they were also used to link presidential power to popular power, with the aim of influencing Congress.

The president demanded "action; and action now." A national emergency, he insisted, required the government to act, and from these circumstances came FDR's New Deal, the birth of the welfare state, and the beginnings of the modern presidency. The New Deal was a combination of legislation, executive orders, and presidential proclamations, dealing with banking reform, Social Security, public relief, public works projects, and a number of other programs. Designed to quickly put people back to work, renew hope, and prime the economic pump, this hodgepodge of programs was more the result of trial and error than any clear economic philosophy. Although the New Deal did not end the Depression, it did renew hope for many and give jobs to some.

The increasing demands on government led to the need for greater institutional support for the presidency. Mushrooming responsibilities required increased staff, and it was in this context that the presidency was transformed from a small, personalized office to a large, "impersonal" institution. At the prodding of the Brownlow Committee, which argued that "the president needs help," an Executive Office of the President was established, beginning the shift to the institutional presidency. Roosevelt's programs met with strong public approval, and though no sudden or dramatic improvement in the economy occurred, a new hope emerged.

Conservatives were generally distressed at Roosevelt's actions during this period, but little in the way of opposition would come from Congress (heavily controlled by the Democrats) or the public (overwhelmingly in favor of the hundred-days legislation). The last hope was the Supreme Court. Several of these bills were challenged and reached the courts for judicial review. Dominated by Republicans, the Supreme Court justices were not thought to be in political sympathy with the New Deal legislation. The question was whether their political preferences would be translated into judicial decisions. The answer was a swift and emphatic yes. By the end of 1936, the Supreme Court had declared unconstitutional nine of the sixteen laws that were the heart of Roosevelt's New Deal legislation.

The Court's decisions were met with harsh criticism by the president, members of Congress, and the general public. Roosevelt felt he had the political clout to do something about the "unresponsive" Court. He was ready to fight back, and after his landslide reelection victory in the 1936 election, Roosevelt struck. Viewing the 1936 election as an endorsement of his New Deal policies, on February 5, 1937, Roosevelt unveiled what became known as his "court-packing plan." This scheme marked a fairly blatant attempt by Roosevelt to force the Supreme Court to change its position and become more amenable to the New Deal legislation. Roosevelt overestimated his electoral mandate and overestimated his political strength, however. The court-packing plan ran into trouble in Congress and with the public. In Congress, the plan hastened the development of the imminently powerful "conservative coalition."

Roosevelt had lost the battle, but what of the war? His court-packing plan may have failed, but in losing the battle he may have won the war with the Supreme Court because between March and June, the Court gave in to Roosevelt on a number of key New Deal issues. The Court approved of the Farm Mortgage Act of 1935, the amended railway Labor Act of 1934, the National Labor Relations Act of 1935, a state minimum wage law, and the Social Security Act of 1935.

By the early 1940s, the Supreme Court had done something of a reversal, when control of the Court passed from Republican to Democratic control and the Court's philosophy changed. Now Roosevelt had a Court more sympathetic to the New Deal. It was now Roosevelt's Court. The earlier Court made a "great retreat." The Court recognized the superior political power the president could wield, and after an initial show of defiance backed down. The new Court would be more to FDR's liking.

If an economic depression were not challenge enough, war loomed in Europe. Roosevelt saw the conflict coming, but the United States was strongly isolationist, with no interest in problems abroad. FDR, ever sensitive to the limits imposed by public opinion, felt he could not move too far too fast. To get too far ahead of public opinion was dangerous in a democracy. So Roosevelt acted— often behind the scenes—to help England (e.g., the Lend-Lease program, which provided US allies with needed supplies), while carefully trying to nudge public opinion in his preferred direction.

On Sunday, December 7, 1941, the Japanese launched a surprise attack on Pearl Harbor, Hawaii. On December 8, Roosevelt asked Congress for a declaration of war against Japan, and three days later, war was declared on Germany and Italy as well, following those nations' declarations of war against the United States.

If the presidency emerged from the Depression stronger and more central to American politics, the Second World War placed Roosevelt and the presidency at the pinnacle of political power. In this, Roosevelt was aided by the now politically compliant Supreme Court. In 1936, the Supreme Court, in *U.S. v. Curtiss-Wright Export Corp.*, upheld a 1934 law authorizing the president to embargo arms sales to countries engaged in conflicts. In and of itself this is not a very significant decision. But the language of the Court's opinion in *Curtiss-Wright* was, to most constitutional scholars, excessive if not downright wrong. A justice referred to the president as the "sole organ" of foreign policy; the executive's authority over foreign affairs was a "plenary and exclusive power." The sweeping language of *Curtiss-Wright*, while criticized by most legal scholars, has been used by nearly every president since Roosevelt to claim extended, if not exclusive, powers in making foreign policy.

The Supreme Court was faced with yet another test of the president's removal power in *Humphrey's Executor v. United States*. William E. Humphrey was chairman of the Federal Trade Commission. President Roosevelt asked for his resignation because, as Roosevelt said, "I do not feel that your mind and my mind go along together on either the policies or the administering of the Federal Trade Commission, and, frankly, I think it best for the people of this country that I should have a full confidence." Humphrey refused to resign, so Roosevelt fired him. Humphrey sued, claiming that the president did not posses unlimited powers of removal over the executive departments and that the act by Roosevelt was purely political (the statute upon which Humphrey based his claim specified "inefficiency, neglect of duty, or malfeasance in office" as grounds for removal by a president). The Supreme Court decided against the president and ruled that the terms of removal for certain officers could be defined by Congress. The Court said: "Whether the power of the President to remove an officer shall prevail over the authority of Congress to condition the power by fixing a definite term and precluding a removal except for the cause, will depend upon the character of the office; the *Myers* decision, affirming the power of the President alone to make the removal, is confined to purely executive officers and that a Federal Trade Commissioner was not such an officer."[17]

When World War II came, Roosevelt, bolstered by public, congressional, and Supreme Court support, articulated an expansive view of the president's wartime power. In his Labor Day speech of September 7, 1942, FDR asserted inherent executive prerogative:

> I ask the Congress to take . . . action by the first of October. Inaction on your part by that date will leave me with an inescapable responsibility to the people of this country to see to it that the war effort is no longer imperiled by threat of economic chaos.
>
> In the event that the Congress should fail to act, and act adequately, I shall accept the responsibility, and I will act. . . .
>
> The President has the powers, under the Constitution and under congressional acts, to take measures necessary to avert a disaster which would interfere with the winning of the war. . . .
>
> The American people can be sure that I will use my powers with a full sense of responsibility to the Constitution and to my country. The American people can also be sure that I shall not hesitate to use every power vested in me to accomplish the defeat of our enemies in any part of the world where our own safety demands such a defeat.

> When the war is won, the powers under which I act automatically revert to the people—to whom they belong.

Congress gave in, allowing FDR to wage war with limited congressional interference.

FDR seemed to argue that during wartime, the Constitution might, to a degree at least, be ignored. Presidents need not adhere to the letter or, at times, even the spirit of the law. World War II brought what constitutional scholar Edward Corwin calls "the most drastic invasion of civil rights in the United States . . . , the most drastic invasion of the rights of citizens of the United States by their own government that has thus far occurred in the history of our nation."[18] Corwin's critical comments derive from the actions taken by the government based upon Executive Order 9066, issued on February 19, 1942. With this order, more than 112,000 Japanese-Americans deemed a danger to national security (more than 80,000 of whom were American citizens) were evacuated from their homes and herded into what were called "relocation centers" situated in the western states. "War," allowed the government to ignore the guarantees within the Constitution and Bill of Rights and to place American citizens in these detention centers.

The Supreme Court was asked to review the legality of the government's actions, and it did so in several cases. The first was *Hirabayashi v. United States*. Hirabayashi was convicted of violating curfew and failure to report to his designated Civil Control Station. The Court decided this case on a very narrow question, avoiding the more important question of the constitutionality of the establishment of the internment centers. In a unanimous decision, the Court ruled that the president and Congress could order a curfew, and the conviction of Hirabayashi was upheld.[19]

In another case, *Korematsu v. United States*, the validity of the evacuation was again challenged. Mr. Korematsu, a resident of San

Leandro, California, refused to leave his home and go to a relocation center. The Court faced a question: was the establishment of the relocation centers a proper exercise of government power? The Supreme Court answered yes. In *Hirabayashi*, the Court avoided the question and thus avoided this extension of presidential power. In *Korematsu* Justice Black wrote:

> We are not unmindful of the hardships imposed . . . upon a large group of American citizens. But hardships are part of war, and war is an aggregation of hardships. All citizens alike, both in and out of uniform, feel the impact of war in greater or lesser measure. Citizenship has its responsibilities as well as its privileges, and in time of war the burden is always heavier. Compulsory exclusion of large groups of citizens from their homes, except under circumstances of direct emergency and peril, is inconsistent with our basic governmental institutions. But when under conditions of our modern warfare our shores are threatened by hostile forces, the power to protect must be commensurate with the threatened danger.[20]

The third case, *Ex Parte Endo*, decided on the same day as *Korematsu*, upheld the right of a Japanese American girl whose loyalty to the United States had been established to a writ of habeas corpus.[21] The writ freed her from a relocation center (two and one-half years after she had filed her petition). Once again, the Court avoided a direct ruling on the constitutionality of the confinement program.

Throughout the war, and in all previous constitutional crises, be they wars, economic crises, or internal insurrections, the president had been expected to "come to the rescue" in our system of government. The public has come to see presidents as saviors, our knights on white horses. In such crises, the power of the president has been expanded to an extent that seems to violate the precepts of constitutional government. The situation during the Second World War was one such crisis. Roosevelt was "given" extraconstitutional powers, and the system revolved around him.

During the war, Roosevelt masterfully led the Allies to victory over the Axis powers. Exercising expansive executive authority, Roosevelt's war leadership further contributed to the developing "president-centric" view of government. The dual emergencies of the Depression and World War II placed the presidency at center stage, but Roosevelt's adept uses of power ensured that a heroic image of the presidency came to dominate the public imagination.

From that point on, the public looked to the president for leadership. The "clerk" presidencies of the Adams, Madison, and Monroe eras had given way. The president was now the recognized leader of the nation, and a "Superman" image developed around the presidency. FDR was the model, and all subsequent presidents were expected to live up to his elevated status. The United States had become a "presidential nation."[22]

The president had become not only leader in-chief but also our national shaman. Through the use of words and symbols, the president was expected to provide meaning, articulate a vision, and define reality for the people. The rhetorical presidency emerged as central to the American system of governing. Recognizing that "the greatest duty of a statesman is to educate," Roosevelt used his public voice to lead and educate as well as to follow public opinion. "The presidency," he told a reporter, "is predominantly a place of moral leadership," and FDR used his office to speak to and, on occasion, lead the public. After Roosevelt, "presidential leadership became, by definition, public leadership."[23]

After Roosevelt, the minimalist state as well as the minimalist presidency no longer seemed possible. Serving during two of the most difficult periods of American history, facing two major crises, Roosevelt redefined both the role of the federal government and the job of the president. He was the architect of the New Deal coalition—a resilient and long-term political realignment—that made the Democrats the nation's majority party, a party that dominated the political landscape for a half century.

Franklin Roosevelt earned his place as one of America's most notable presidents. He quickly became an American icon, along with Washington, Jefferson, and Lincoln. He enlarged the presidency and expanded the scope of the federal government. He was an event-making president.

The Postwar and Cold War Presidency Emerges

The Great Depression added new responsibilities to the federal government and new powers to the presidency. World War II did the same. After the war, world leadership also added to the stature and power of the presidency. Subsequently, the Cold War and the creation of the national security state gave the presidency even more expansive powers.

The United States emerged from World War II as the dominant or hegemonic power of the West. As the "only" true superpower, the United States had sobering responsibilities, as well as significant opportunities. Yet it was not long before US world leadership was challenged. The Soviet Union, though not possessing the power or status of the United States, nonetheless began to clash with the United States over control of the postwar world. A bipolar conflict, known as the Cold War, quickly enveloped the globe.

To meet the challenge of the Cold War, the United States set up a permanent wartime economy, created a national security state, and gave to the president vast powers to fight this ongoing Cold War. The republic had been overtaken by empire. The United States of the Cold War era was a vastly different nation from the one FDR governed in 1933. The Depression and New Deal led to the acceptance of a larger, more positive governmental approach to economic intervention and management. World War II centralized production and put the economy on a war footing; the public had also come to expect, even demand, strong, assertive presidential leadership. When in the immediate aftermath of World War II, the Cold War engulfed the world, it seemed only natural to once again turn to the institution "created" by FDR to see us through the new Cold War crisis. And it would fall on Roosevelt's successor to meet this challenge.

Harry Truman (1945–1953) inherited the presidency near the end of World War II.[24] If the end was in sight, however, the war was far from over. Important decisions about the conduct of the war had yet to be made, including what to do about the atomic bomb. And once the war ended, the United States was thrust into a position of global leadership and had to respond to the growing conflict with the Soviet Union. Truman's new responsibilities were truly awesome. Not only was he expected to bring a successful conclusion to the war, but he also had to decide whether to drop "the bomb," how to guide the nation to demobilization, how to deal with postwar fallout in Europe, how to create a new postwar world, how to respond to a new antagonist, and how to fill FDR's shoes.

When Germany surrendered on May 8, 1945, it became clear that the Soviet Union intended to continue occupying Eastern Europe and to maintain control of the eastern portion of Germany. In July 1945, Truman met with Stalin at the Potsdam Conference to discuss this and other issues, but there was no positive resolution. During the meeting, Truman gave the go-ahead to use the atomic bomb on Hiroshima and, if necessary, Nagasaki, in hopes of hastening Japanese surrender. The bombings, on August 6 and August 9, led to the deaths of more than 120,000 and forced the Japanese into unconditional surrender on August 14, 1945.

As the problems of the world war ended, the problems of the nascent Cold War began. Soviet leader Joseph Stalin quickly imposed communist governments in Eastern Europe. Several Western European nations appeared on the verge of collapse and perhaps communist takeover. In an effort to bolster noncommunist governments, in March 1947, Truman promised support for any nation struggling against communist takeover. The Truman Doctrine initially involved emergency aid to Greece and Turkey. The Marshall Plan followed, an ambitious effort to rebuild Western Europe. Then the North Atlantic Treaty Organization (NATO), the US-Western European security pact, was created. This was the beginning of a "containment" policy designed to confine the spread of Soviet influence around the globe. This policy was followed, more or less, by every US president until the collapse of the Soviet Union. It was this program, established by Harry S Truman, that ended up winning the Cold War.

Another result of these tactics used during the Cold War was the creation of a national security state. The National Security Act of 1947 reorganized the military under the control of the secretary of defense and created the National Security Council and the Central Intelligence Agency under the control of the president. The president was placed squarely at the head of this new and powerful national security state. And in order for the presidency to grow in power, presidents needed to institutionalize, that is, build into the minds of the public and Congress a set of expectations regarding the new powers of the office. The creation and institutionalization of the national security state greatly expanded the powers, responsibilities, and independence of the presidency in dealing with foreign affairs. "I make American foreign policy," Truman told the Jewish War Veterans in 1948. It seemed a preposterous claim of independent power, made all the more preposterous by its accuracy.

Since a hot war between the Soviet Union and the United States was, in a nuclear age, far too dangerous to contemplate, smaller surrogate wars were fought around the globe. One of the first such clashes took place in Korea. North Korea, controlled by the communists, invaded South Korea in 1950. President Truman called for a "police" action to repel the North. Truman chose to order US forces into combat on his own claimed constitutional authority and did not ask Congress for a declaration of war or authorization to commit US troops to combat. Senator James P. Kem (R–MO) orated in the Senate chamber, "I notice that in the president's statement he says, 'I have ordered the fleet to prevent any attack on Formosa.' Does that mean he has arrogated to himself the authority of declaring war?" Indeed, that is precisely what Truman had done. In the tense atmosphere of the Cold War, the president grabbed power and claimed a new, unilateral authority that he said was grounded in the Constitution. Congress wilted. The war power now seemed to belong to the president.

But the Korean War was a stalemate, and soon the president and General Douglas MacArthur, the United Nations commander in Korea, were at odds. As MacArthur became more open in his criticism of Truman, going so far as to directly challenge the president, Truman felt he had no other option than to fire the popular general. He did so, and a political firestorm swept the nation, but Truman stuck to his guns. In his diary, Truman called the public reaction to his firing of MacArthur "quite an explosion." But with or without public approval, Truman knew he was right—a general could not undermine the commander in chief. Truman said: "I wonder how far Moses would have gone if he had taken a poll in Egypt? I wonder would Jesus Christ have preached if He had taken a poll in the land of Israel? Where would the Reformation have gone if Martin Luther had taken a poll? It isn't polls or public opinion of the moment that counts. It is right and wrong, and leadership—men with fortitude, honesty and a belief in the right that makes epochs in the history of the world."[25]

In 1952, the Korean War raged on, and in an effort to avoid a steel strike that might have adversely affected the war effort, Truman issued an executive order calling for the government seizure of the steel mills. A major constitutional controversy ensued. Claiming "implied" or inherent powers during an (undeclared) emergency, Truman felt confident that the Supreme Court would uphold the seizure. But the Supreme Court, in *Youngstown Sheet & Tube Co. v. Sawyer* (1952), found against Truman. Justice Hugo Black argued in his opinion for the Court that Truman's order was a de facto statute (law) and that the Constitution did not provide the president with the lawmaking power: "In the framework of our Constitution, the President's power to see that the laws are faithfully executed refutes the idea that he is to be a lawmaker. The Constitution limits his functions in the lawmaking process to the recommending of laws he thinks wise and the vetoing of laws he thinks bad. And the Constitution is neither silent nor equivocal about who shall make laws which the President is to execute. The first section of the first article says that 'All legislative powers herein granted shall be vested in a Congress of the United States.'" Truman could not, the Court argued, act alone. The Court's rebuff of a claim of presidential authority was significant, for rarely did it curb presidential power in the realm of foreign affairs, especially during wartime, declared or otherwise. There were, after all, some limits on the expansive Cold War presidency.

During the Truman administration, several new executive agencies were created, including the Council of Economic Advisers, the Atomic Energy Commission, the National Security Council, the Central Intelligence Agency, and the National Science Foundation. These agencies strengthened the president's control over policy decisions and gave the president access to information vital to controlling the nation's political agenda.

President Truman exercised bold, innovative leadership in tough times. To Truman, the presidency was the center of the American (and international) universe. To drive the point home, a sign on his White House desk read: "The Buck Stops Here."

During Truman's presidency, Germany and Japan surrendered, the United States dropped the first atomic bombs, a winning Cold War policy took shape, the post–World War II moved beyond the horrors of war, Europe was rebuilt, communism was resisted, NATO was created, the Marshall Plan and Truman Doctrine were implemented, and civil rights became a national issue. But there were also setbacks. The Korean War was a stalemate, Truman's relationship with the Republican Congress was rocky, Senator Joseph McCarthy threatened American liberties, and China fell to the communists.

Truman took America and the West into a new and dangerous Cold War age, protected and strengthened the world's fragile democracies, held the ambitions of the Soviet Union in check, and pressed for reforms at home. "I must confess," Winston Churchill told Truman at the end of his presidency, "I held you in very low regard. . . . I loathed you taking the place of Franklin Roosevelt. I misjudged you badly. . . . [Y]ou more than anyone have saved Western Civilization."[26]

By this time the United States had a big government and a big presidency. And the big presidency was generally celebrated by the public as well as the academic community. Edward S. Corwin in his highly regarded text *The President: Office and Powers* (1940) states: "The history of the presidency is a history of aggrandizement, but the story is a highly discontinuous one. Of the thirty-three individuals who have filled the office not more than one in three has contributed to the development of its powers. . . . So the force of Precedents established by a forceful or politically successful personality in the office are available to less gifted successors, and permanently so because of the difficulty with which the Constitution is amended."[27]

Another of the prominent academic cheerleaders is Clinton Rossiter. Widely read and highly influential, Rossiter presents a heroic portrait of the American presidency, calling it "one of the few truly successful institutions created by men in the endless quest for the blessings of free government." He admits his "own feeling of veneration, if not exactly reverence, for the authority and dignity of the Presidency." Rossiter later refers to the president as "a kind of magnificent lion who can roam widely and do great deeds so long as he does not try to break loose from his broad reservation." The "final definition" of a "strong and successful" president is, he notes, "one who knows just how far he can go in the direction he wants to go," and, therefore, "the power of the Presidency moves as a mighty host only *with* the grain of liberty and morality."[28]

The academic cult of the presidency continued to grow with the influential work of Richard Neustadt. His 1960 book *Presidential Power* called for an activist president who knew how to get and use power. Arguing that the strictly constitutional presidency was rather anemic, Neustadt called on the president to fully use the personal levers of power to elevate his prestige or "reputation," especially within the Washington axis. As "the probabilities of power do not derive from the literary theory of the Constitution," presidents must creatively use the political levers of power to overcome their constitutional limitations. Neustadt saw the power to persuade as the president's chief source of influence:

> The power to persuade is the power to bargain. Status and authority yield bargaining advantages. But in a government of "separated institutions sharing powers," they yield them to all sides. With the array of vantage points at his disposal, a President may be far more persuasive than his logic or his charm could make him. But outcomes are not guaranteed by his advantages. There remain the counter pressures those whom he would influence can bring to bear on him from vantage points at their disposal. Command has limited utility; persuasion becomes give-and-take. It is well that

the White House holds the vantage point it does. In such a business any President may need them all—and more.[29]

When Things Fall Apart

The sudden, tragic death of President John F. Kennedy put Lyndon Baines Johnson (1963–1969) (LBJ) in the White House.[30] Johnson was an experienced legislator and a larger than life character. He was an overbearing, domineering man of monumental ambition, an earthy sense of humor, and a need to be the center of attention. Johnson was also considered a legislative master. In 1965 and 1966, he and the Eighty-Ninth Congress passed a number of important pieces of legislation bills: Medicare, Medicaid, the Civil Rights Act, the War on Poverty, the Air Pollution Control Act, and the Elementary and Secondary Education Act. They also created the Departments of Transportation and Housing and Urban Development. The number of major bills passed was astonishing. While the table may have been set by Kennedy, and the political environment greased by the tragic death of President Kennedy, it was Johnson who succeeded in getting the landmark legislation through Congress.

Johnson's Great Society was second only to the New Deal in size and importance. "There is but one way for a president to deal with the Congress," Johnson said, "and that is continuously, incessantly, and without interruption. If it's going to work, the relationship between the president and Congress has got to be almost incestuous."[31]

Yet just when the public seemed lulled into a false sense of complacency and security concerning the inherent benevolence of presidential power, things began to change. They changed quickly and dramatically, and it started with Vietnam. US involvement in Vietnam began quietly, escalated slowly, and eventually turned into a tragedy. By 1966, the United States was engaged in a war it could not win and from which it could not honorably withdraw. It was a "presidential war," and it brought the Johnson administration to its knees and compelled LBJ not to seek reelection in 1968.

As US involvement escalated and victory seemed out of reach, blame was placed directly at the feet of President Johnson. By the time Johnson came to office, presidents had been setting policy in Vietnam for roughly twenty years, virtually unencumbered by Congress. It was the president calling the shots. The tragedy of Lyndon Johnson is that after such a sterling start, after such great success, the blunder of Vietnam would overwhelm him and the nation. From such great heights, the president fell to such tragic depths, and the nation was torn apart.

The glue that bound Americans together as a nation had lost its adhesiveness, and in its place, divisiveness, demonstrations, protests, and conflict overtook the nation. The strong presidency, long believed to be the savior of America, now seemed too powerful, too dangerous, too unchecked—in short, a threat. After years of calls for "more power to the president," by the late 1960s the plea was to rein in the overly powerful leviathan in the White House. Presidential power now seemed like poison. It was a rude awakening. All the hopes, the trust, the expectations that had been placed before the presidency from FDR on were shattered. Johnson was compelled not to seek reelection in 1968 when faced with the certainty of electoral defeat.

Richard M. Nixon (1969–1974), the first and only president to resign from office (to avoid impeachment and conviction) for abuse of power and criminal activity, was deeply insecure, vindictive, combative, and morally obtuse.[32] He was brilliant, but deeply flawed. An innovative foreign policy strategist, he was a small, hurtful, angry man. He remains an enigma and a maddening mix of admirable and despicable qualities.

The Nixon years were a time of dramatic, bold, innovative approaches and overtures in the area of foreign affairs, a time when the conventional wisdom was challenged and conventional solutions were eschewed for a new strategic approach to foreign policy. It was an era that brought about an opening of relations with China, détente with the Soviet Union, and a strategic-arms limitation agreement with the Soviets. It was a period when America's military involvement in Vietnam and Southeast Asia was expanded, then finally ended, and when a relatively new strategic orientation was introduced into American foreign policy thinking.

Under Richard Nixon and his national security adviser, Henry Kissinger, a reexamination of the United States' role in the world produced a different strategic vision. There was recognition of the changing capacity of the United States, recognition of the limits of power, and recognition that the nation's strategic vision should attempt to match its capabilities. Had it not been for Watergate and the self-destruction of the Nixon presidency, there is no telling how the early stages of the Nixon foreign policy revolution might have impacted the United States and the world.

The world was becoming more complex, more interdependent, and less amenable to US dominance. Amid this policy incoherence and confusion, the time seemed ripe for a fundamental change in American foreign policy. But how should the United States respond to this changing world? Gone were the days when American power seemed capable of solving virtually any problem simply by overwhelming them with America's superior economic or military might. The world had changed; the United States had changed. Absent overwhelming resource superiority, the United States had to be more careful, selective, and creative. But how does one adjust responsibilities to match declining power while still exerting hegemonic control?[33]

Nixon and Kissinger attempted to deal with relative decline by developing slightly more modest international commitments (the Nixon Doctrine), developing a new international system (Nixon's ambitious "Grand Design" or new "structure of peace"), exerting personal international leadership (what was referred to as shuttle diplomacy), and refashioning US relationships with the two most powerful communist nations (détente with the Soviet Union, opening the door to China). Scholar Robert Osgood has called the new strategy "military retrenchment without political disengagement."[34] Nixon attempted to deal with the overextension of American power not by retreating from American globalism, but by starting an orderly, controlled readjustment, a measured devolution.[35] The United States would have to settle for less, set clearer priorities, and redefine the national interest. But could this be done while still playing the role of hegemon?

Nixon attempted to implement what he called a new and ambitious "Grand Strategy" for foreign affairs. Like so many other aspects of his presidency, however, the grand designs gave way to petty politics, and Nixon's ambitious plans were eventually crushed by the weight of the Watergate scandal.

At home, because the opposition party controlled Congress, Nixon devised an "administrative strategy" to govern.[36] Where possible, he attempted to bypass Congress and use administrative discretion as much as possible. This administrative strategy was an innovation that would later be used by President Reagan and others with great success. The swelling of the administrative presidency further added to the tools available for presidential leadership.

It is impossible to discuss the Nixon presidency without covering Watergate, the most serious scandal in the history of US presidential politics. This scandal was unusual because for the first time in history the president himself was deeply involved in the crimes of his administration. Watergate was a different kind of scandal—but then, Richard Nixon was a different kind of president.

Watergate is a generic term that originally referred to the break-in at the Democratic National Committee headquarters located at the Washington, DC, Watergate office complex, but it has come to be an umbrella term, under which a wide range of crimes and improper acts are included. Watergate caused the downfall of President Nixon. It led to jail sentences for more than a dozen of the highest-ranking officials of the administration. It was a constitutional crisis and a traumatic experience for the nation.

As the Watergate investigations drew the noose tighter and tighter around the president's neck, it became increasingly clear that President Nixon would be impeached by the House and convicted by the Senate. The Supreme Court decision in *U.S. v. Nixon* (1974) ordered the president to release White House tape recordings (while also adding to the power of the presidency by establishing judicial recognition of limited "executive privilege") that clearly established the fact that Nixon had been actively involved in criminal behavior. From that point on, what little support Nixon had very quickly evaporated. To escape impeachment, Nixon resigned from office on August 9, 1974. He is the only president to resign his office. The House Judiciary Committee ended up approving three articles of impeachment against President Nixon. (See Text Box 4.1.)

The aftermath of Watergate led to a sharp decline in the powers of the presidency and also to a resurgence of congressional power. It was a presidency-bashing age. As a result first of Vietnam, then of Watergate, the people's white knight had turned into an imperial president. The presidency had become a danger to the republic, using its powers not for the public good but for self-aggrandizement.

Reacting against the perceived excesses of power in the Johnson and Nixon presidencies, Congress attempted to reassert itself by taking a series of presidency-curbing steps, the most notable of which was the passage of the War Powers Act, an attempt (with little success) to curb the president's war powers. The presidency-curbing era also ushered in a period in which the public did an about-face regarding their support of presidents and the presidency. Now, virtually

ARTICLE OF IMPEACHMENT AGAINST RICHARD M. NIXON

Article I

In his conduct of the office of President of the United States, Richard M. Nixon, in violation of his constitutional oath faithful to execute the office of President of the United States and, to the best of his ability, preserve, protect and defend the Constitution of the United States, and, in violation of his constitutional duty to take care that the laws be faithfully executed, has prevented, obstructed, and impeded the administration of justice, in that:

On June 17, 1972, and prior thereto, agents of the Committee for the Reelection of the President committed unlawful entry of the headquarters of the Democratic National Committee in Washington, District of Columbia, for the purpose of securing political intelligence. Subsequent thereto, Richard M. Nixon, using the powers of his high office, engaged personally and through his subordinates and agents, in a course of conduct or plan designed to delay, impede, and obstruct the investigation of such unlawful entry; to cover up, conceal and protect those responsible; and to conceal the existence and scope of other unlawful covert activities.

Article II

Using the powers of the office of President of the United States, Richard M. Nixon, in violation of his constitutional oath faithfully to execute the office of President of the United States and, to the best of his ability, preserve, protect, and defend the Constitution of the United States, and in disregard of his constitutional duty to take care that the laws be faithfully executed, has repeatedly engaged in conduct violating the constitutional rights of citizens, impairing the due and proper administration of justice and the conduct of lawful inquiries, or contravening the laws governing the agencies of the executive branch and the purposes of these agencies.

Article III

In his conduct of the office of President of the United States, Richard M. Nixon, contrary to his oath faithfully to execute the office of President of the United States and, to the best of his ability, preserve, protect, and defend the Constitution of the United States, and in violation of his constitutional duty to take care that the laws be faithfully executed, has failed without lawful cause or excuse to produce papers and things as directed by duly authorized subpoenas issued by the Committee on the Judiciary of the House of Representatives. . . . In refusing to produce these papers and things, Richard M. Nixon, substituted his judgment as to what materials were necessary for the inquiry, interposed the powers of the Presidency against the lawful subpoenas of the House of Representatives, thereby assuming to himself functions and judgments necessary to the exercise of the sole power or impeachment vested by the Constitution in the House of Representatives.

In all of this, Richard M. Nixon has acted in a manner contrary to his trust as President and subversive of constitutional government, to the great prejudice of the cause of law and justice, and to the manifest injury of the people of the United States. Wherefore, Richard M. Nixon, by such conduct, warrants impeachment and trial, and removal from office.*

*Report of the Committee on the Judiciary,
US House of Representatives, August 20, 1974

---

all presidential acts were suspect, virtually no support was given for presidential initiatives, and a weak-presidency model (though not a strong-Congress model) prevailed. A new breed of activist Democrats was elected to the Congress. Weaned not on FDR's greatness but on Johnson's and Nixon's excesses, this new generation was far less deferential to presidents, less willing to bow to claims of presidential prerogative, and more willing to challenge presidents directly. As a result, the legislative initiatives of Presidents Ford and Carter would fall victim to Congress's more skeptical attitude toward presidential power.[37] It was during this period that historian Arthur M. Schlesinger Jr. wrote *The Imperial Presidency*, an assault on a presidency that Schlesinger believed had grown above the law.[38]

After the crisis of Vietnam, the scandal of Watergate, and the lackluster presidencies of Ford and Carter, the nation began to forget about the problems of presidential power, and as problems mounted, a hunger for leadership emerged. The people wanted a strong leader, someone who could solve problems and flex America's muscles. Enter Ronald Reagan (1981–1989), a presidential knight in shining armor.[39] Reagan seemed to be everything his predecessors Ford and Carter were not: strong and self-assured, a leader. He made bold promises, spoke in grand terms, and created high expectations. He attempted to return America to an era of grandeur and power.

At first, Reagan took Washington by storm. Claiming a bold electoral mandate and focusing on several key economic items, Reagan managed to get several of his top agenda items enacted into law. Yet after an impressive start, Reagan faltered. Initial success in dealing with Congress gave way to frustration and defeat. The president could not overcome the system's roadblocks, and unwilling to accept the limits placed upon the office, he and members of his administration went beyond the law and abused power.

Ronald Reagan's engaging personality and ready wit helped make him personally popular, yet while his borrow-borrow, spend-spend approach to policy added to America's military might, it also left the nation on the brink of economic insolvency. During the Reagan presidency, the United States went from being the world's largest creditor and lender nation in 1980 to becoming the world's largest debtor and borrower nation in 1988.

Reagan was known as the "Great Communicator." His use of the rhetorical and symbolic powers of the office enhanced his image and added to his power. He had a clear message to communicate, and he communicated that message with force and clarity. He came to office challenging the policies of the New Deal era, and he wanted to undo the Roosevelt revolution and replace it with a Reagan revolution: less government, lower taxes, a bigger defense budget, cuts in social welfare spending, and cuts in government regulations on business.

Above all other postwar presidents, Ronald Reagan used television as a tool of leadership. He attempted a direct connection to the people via carefully crafted speeches, painstakingly stage-managed theatrics, and exploitation of his winning personality. This plebiscitary form of leadership "exposes citizens to the sort of public figures who will exploit their impatience with the difficult tasks involved in sustaining a healthy constitutional democracy."[40]

Reagan, like Nixon, asserted an administrative strategy of governing in hopes of wresting control of policy from Congress. He had more success than Nixon, partly because his administration insisted that all appointees pass a rigid litmus test to prove loyalty to Reagan and his program. Yet in the long run, this approach would end up getting the administration into trouble. Reagan increased the military budget and engaged in a war of words with the Soviet Union, calling them "the evil empire." The president was determined to roll back Soviet influence, especially in this hemisphere. That led him to overreach badly and led to the most serious crisis of his presidency: the Iran-Contra scandal.

In November 1986, a Lebanese publication broke a story accusing the Reagan administration of trading arms for American hostages being held in Iran. Reagan had publicly condemned dealing with terrorists and pressured US allies not to deal with them either. But the Reagan administration had been trading arms for hostages—or at least trying to do so. Led by the cartoonish character Lieutenant Colonel Oliver "Ollie" North, a Reagan operative in the national security arena, the administration formed a plan whereby the United States gave Iran much-needed arms and the Iranians promised to release the US hostages. There was, however, one catch: when the weapons were delivered, the Iranians did not release any hostages. So the United States sent *more* arms, until the Iranians finally released one hostage. But for every hostage released, another one was taken. The absurd pas de deux lasted for two years, as the United States continued to play the fool to the Iranians.

The arms sales made hefty profits for the United States. But what to do with the illegal profits from these illegal arms sales? The Keystone Kops in the White House decided to use the profits to fund the "Contras," the right-wing Nicaraguan rebels fighting the Sandanista (Marxist) government of Nicaragua. This was done in direct violation of US law. The Boland Amendment prevented any such aid to the Contras, but Reagan disagreed with this law.

When eventually caught, the president engaged in a performance worthy of the Marx brothers. Reagan went back and forth in his statements about his involvement in the Iran-Contra scandal. On July 8, 1985, he called Iran part of a confederation of "outlaw states run by the strangest collection of misfits, Looney Tunes, and squalid criminals since the advent of the Third Reich." But over time, his story kept changing:

> "We did not—repeat—did not trade weapons or anything else for hostages."
> —November 13, 1986
> "I don't think a mistake was made."
> —November 19, 1986
> "I'm not going to lie about that. I didn't make a mistake."
> —November 24, 1986
> "It's obvious that the execution of these policies was flawed, and mistakes were made."
> —December 6, 1986

"I told the American people I did not trade arms for hostages. My heart and my best intentions still tell me that's true. But the facts and the evidence tell me it is not. . . . What began as a strategic opening to Iran deteriorated in its implementation into trading arms for hostages."
—March 4, 1987

When the Iran-Contra scandal broke, Reagan seemed politically as well as personally paralyzed. He became so withdrawn that chief of staff Howard Baker even considered invoking the Twenty-Fifth Amendment to remove a disabled president.[41]

Ronald Reagan left a mixed and in many ways confusing legacy. He helped revive the spirit and confidence of the American people. His policies accelerated the decline of the Soviet Union, and he used the rhetorical aspects of the presidency to full effect. And he helped shift the center of political discourse to the right of the ideological scale. Yet the Reagan years also left astronomical budget deficits, a wider gap between the rich and poor, a legacy of sleaze, the Iran-Contra scandal, and an aloof and disengaged management style. Reagan was a good leader (of a conservative movement), but not a very good president. He asserted a great deal of executive prerogative, but did so in a manner that far exceeded the bounds of the law. In the end, he left the presidency and the nation weaker than when he took office.

During the Reagan presidency, conservatives, who had long been critics of big government and the big presidency, did a 180 on both issues. In Reagan, conservatives saw what a big presidency could mean for their conservative cause. Conservative commentators such as Terry Eastland eschewed the traditional conservative positions as poison and embraced presidential power as savior.[42] Thus, during the Reagan years, the presidency grew, as did the size of the federal government, as did the size of the federal deficit.

Conclusion

The fortunes of individual presidents rose and fell in this era, as did the power of the presidency itself. Yet if presidential power was in flux, the overall trend was toward increased power. Several presidents challenged the cooperative-consensus model established by the US Constitution. But no president went as far—in word or deed—as would George W. Bush, the subject of our next chapter.

5

9/11 and the Presidency

THE MOST DANGEROUS BRANCH?
OR, L'ÉTAT C'EST MOI, 2001–PRESENT

If the overall trend of America's political history is a rise in presidential power over time, that increase in power has, for the most part, remained encased in the web established by the Constitution. Presidents found new tools along the way, stretched limits here and there, yet were always cognizant of the overriding system of checks and balances and the rule of law.

Even as the powers of the presidency grew, presidents were still—for the most part—reluctant to make bold claims of having unilateral or constitutional authority to act on their own, absent some form of congressional authorization. They remained true in word, if not always in deed, to the higher authority of the Constitution and recognized that theirs was an office limited by shared and blended powers. Lincoln, as he acted boldly, still recognized that only Congress could legitimize his emergency actions taken on the grounds of necessity. The same was true of FDR during the Depression and World War II.

The first real threat to the constitutional integrity of the system, the first serious act of constitutional violence, was Harry Truman's claim that he had plenary constitutional authority—without Congress—to lead the nation into war. This marked a new and dangerous chapter in president-congressional relations and threatened the sanctity of the rule of law. The second great threat was Richard Nixon's bogus and imperial claim that "when the president does it, that means it is not illegal." One would have thought that his resignation in disgrace would have put an end to such presidential pretensions, yet this sentiment would be revived a quarter century later in the presidency of George W. Bush.

The most serious threat to constitutional integrity came in the weeks after the 9/11 attack against the United States. The actions of the Bush administration ran contrary to the law—as the Republican-controlled Supreme Court said on several occasions—but it was the even bolder claims of constitutional authority by the president and his lawyers that jeopardized constitutionalism and the rule of law. These claims of the Bush administration give pause to ask: Is the presidency dangerous to democracy? And is the presidency "the most dangerous branch"?[1]

The American presidency, invented in 1787 by men intent on rejecting the divine right of kings and rule by "one" man, established a system of limited government under the rule of law based on a constitution that separated powers within a regime of checks and balances in which the president was to preside as but one of three separate branches, a system that over time has morphed or evolved into a presidential government that resembles the imperial government the framers rejected and overthrew. Have we come full circle from a hereditary monarch to an elected monarch, with presidents of imperial proportions? For the first time in our history, we face the grave threat that the presidency is becoming unmoored from the separation-of-powers system. A unilateral presidency is what the framers rejected. It was—and is—a threat to the republic.

Terrorism's Impact on Presidential Power

When crisis strikes, Americans look to the president as their savior. This is precisely what happened on September 11, 2001. When the planes struck the Twin Towers, Americans turned almost instinctively to their president. "Do something!" they seemed to plead. In the confusing and frightening wake of the collapsed towers, a political vacuum was created. The public expected the president fill that void, and President Bush did.

Almost immediately, the White House leapt into action, Congress pulled back, the courts waited silently on the sidelines, and the public threw its collective weight behind the president. The executive branch mobilized the machinery of government to respond to this new threat. Was this a case of the president acting within the accepted sphere of his authority, or did President Bush respond in an extraconstitutional manner? If the presidency had become an imperial institution, it was in part because we demanded it become one.

The initial optimism in the war against terror was based on the speed with which the United States and a large coalition of other nations seemed to defeat the Taliban government in Afghanistan. American power—and presidential leadership—were leading the United States to victory. Through a series of steps, the administration moved to secure the homeland and prosecute a war against terrorism internationally. It was an ambitious effort, yet one that seemed to get off to a good start.

Then things went terribly wrong. The war of necessity in Afghanistan became a war of choice in Iraq as the Bush administration, not content merely to go after the terrorists, decided that an opportunity existed to take military action against "bigger fish." The administration harbored grander ambitions. The president wanted to finish the job his father had begun a decade earlier and "take out" Saddam Hussein as ruler of Iraq. To do this, the administration conveyed false information and bogus intelligence reports to the public and other governments.

Misleading the nation into war was initially not a political problem. Militarily, the assault in Iraq went quickly and smoothly. The United States and a very few allies toppled the Iraqi government, arrested Saddam Hussein, and on May 2, 2003, the president flew in the copilot seat of a Navy S-3B Viking fighter jet onto the USS *Lincoln* aircraft carrier, where he gave a rousing speech in the shadow of a huge "MISSION ACCOMPLISHED" banner and announced that "major combat operations in Iraq have ended. In the battle of Iraq, the United States and our allies have prevailed." Not quite. Over four years, and more than four thousand American lives later, the mission had morphed into a civil war with brutal sectarian violence. The United States scrambled for a strategy to respond to events on the ground. It was a bloody mess.

This brief history reveals the good and bad sides of vesting unchecked power in one man during a crisis. Bold leadership can solve problems, but it can also create a mess. It can get the machinery of government moving in order to act swiftly to meet a grave threat, but it can also become a grave threat itself by abusing that power or making avoidable blunders that plunge the nation into catastrophe. Trusting one man has its costs.

The American system is thus highly vulnerable to the benefits as well as the pitfalls of one-man rule. It wasn't supposed to be that way. The framers of the United States Constitution sought to avoid the one-man rule they had deemed so tyrannical when power was exercised by the British king against the colonies. The United States was supposed to be different.

George W. Bush Fights a War Against Terrorism

The debate over presidential power after 9/11 was fought largely between what we might call the *presidentialist* camp, which sees an expansive presidency, and the *constitutionalist* camp, which argues that the Constitution calls for a sharing of power by the president and Congress. Emboldened by 9/11, the presidentialists began to make claims for the presidency that defied logic and ran counter to the overwhelming weight of evidence.[2]

Armed with overwhelming public support for an aggressive response, cognizant of the unlikelihood of an independent congressional response, and unconcerned with the potential checking power of the courts, these presidentialists pushed forward their claims of presidential power, encouraging an expansive use of this newly empowered office as a tool to further a conservative international agenda. Many of these conservatives or (neoconservatives), who attacked the use of presidential power when in the hands of Democrats,[3] now called for unchecked presidential power in the hands of the Republican, Bush. In politics, so many actions are opportunity based. September 11 created an opportunity for conservative presidentialists to seize power and pursue their political and policy objectives virtually unchecked.[4] And they were not shy about using this power.

How did conservatives, so suspicious of centralized authority and big government, embrace a brand of imperial presidential power that was anything but conservative? They would present a theory of presidential power that ran counter to the expressed views of the framers. They promoted what they called the "unitary executive" view of presidential power.

The Unitary Executive: Born, or Reborn?

The unitary executive is a model of presidential power that posits that "all" executive powers belong exclusively to the president.[5] In its most expansive form, the unitary executive sees presidential authority as disembodied from the separation of powers and checks and balances, and thus would be in apparent contradiction to the original model of constitutionalism envisioned by the framers.

The proponents of the unitary executive theory of presidential power trace this view back to the founding era and to Alexander Hamilton, but it was never the dominant or even the accepted position of the framers, nor was it written into the Constitution. And in his writings in *The Federalist Papers*, Hamilton *does not* articulate a vision of executive power that matches the unilateral claims of presidential power made by today's unitary executive advocates. While "necessity" may make the unitary executive an attractive alternative to the constitutional presidency in an age of terrorism, such necessity does not make the unitary executive constitutional.[6]

If, as the Bush administration asserted, the war against terrorism will be a war without end, and if in war "necessity" trumps the Constitution, giving the president a vastly increased reservoir of power, it is imperative that we come to grips with the potential threats the war powers pose to the constitutional republic. If presidential power is used too hesitantly or unwisely, the security and future of the nation may be put at risk; if used too aggressively or too expansively, the security of the constitutional republic is endangered. How well or poorly this paradox is resolved will determine what type of polity we will have and what type of people we will be for the coming decades.

Constitutionally, the scope of a president's war powers are somewhat ill-defined. Historically, the president has been granted wide authority to meet crises and war; however, such authority is not absolute. While the Constitution cannot be a suicide pact, neither can it be a meaningless piece of paper. And although, as Supreme Court Justice Frank Murphy wrote in *Hirabayashi v. U.S.*, war gives the president "authority to exercise measures of control over persons and property which would not in all cases be permissible in normal times," such powers are not without limits. As the Supreme Court reminded in *United States v. Robel* (1967), "Even the war power does not remove constitutional limitations safeguarding essential liberties." And roughly forty years later, Justice Sandra Day O'Connor wrote in *Hamdi v. Rumsfeld* (2004) that "a state of war is not a blank check for the president" and that the commander-in-chief powers do not give the president the authority to "turn our system of checks and balances on its head."[7]

The modern academic cache for the unitary executive grew primarily out of several law journal articles touting a new, originalist construction of the robust version of president power.[8] Yet even many conservatives are skeptical of this newly discovered originalist construction of broad presidential power.

The Bush administration relied on the unitary theory to claim broad powers for the president. The post-9/11 presidency of George W. Bush was a bold, muscle-flexing, assertive, and in some ways unilateral presidency. Initially, the Bush administration was both powerful and popular. But as the fallout of the administration's actions in Iraq and elsewhere took center stage and as the sentiment of the public, our allies, and political opponents soured, the Bush presidency was compelled to move beyond mere assertions of power and present a political and intellectual justification for its unilateral actions. The result was the "unitary executive." While the roots of the unitary executive in practice trace back to the administration of Ronald Reagan, it was not until the Bush administration that this theory became more fully developed and implemented.[9]

The Crisis Leadership of George W. Bush

In response to the 9/11 attacks against the United States, the Bush administration argued that a wholly new approach to foreign policy was needed to meet the new dangers posed by a new type of emergency. The president declared an international war against a new enemy, terrorism. The United States passed the USA Patriot Act, created the Department of Homeland Security, adopted a doctrine of "first strike" or preventative/preemptive war, began a war against the Taliban government in Afghanistan, pursued the al-Qaeda terrorist network, and later launched a war against Saddam Hussein in Iraq. The United States was "at war," and George W. Bush was, as he often reminded the public, "a war president."

Several of the president's policies were controversial. On his own claimed authority, he established military tribunals, set questionable standards for determining "enemy combatants," authorized what may be defined as torture, set up a detention center in Cuba at Guantánamo Bay, began a policy of "extraordinary renditions," established an illegal National Security Agency eavesdropping program domestically, denied US citizens habeas corpus, and denied citizens access to attorneys, all without congressional approval. It was a breathtaking exercise of unilateral presidential power.

Perhaps most unsettling is the administration's assertion that in war, a president's actions are nonreviewable by the other branches. This self-serving claim bristles with both institutional and personal arrogance, and if left unchallenged, it eviscerates our system of checks and balances. A president accountable to no one but himself smacks of monarchical pretensions.

While his popularity hovered in the 80 percent range, the president felt emboldened by a clear mission, and he possessed unrivaled political capital. Yet his high power level did not last. As the war in Iraq took a turn for the worse, as examples of the torture of US prisoners came to light, as memos defending torture and extralegal authority of the president were leaked, as news of "extraordinary renditions" was revealed, as the stories out of the US detention center in Guantánamo Bay surfaced, as the shocking photos of Abu Ghraib were released, and as the president's plans for military tribunals and denial of Geneva Convention rights became known, the administration was backed into a defensive posture. Could all these acts emanate solely from the executive branch? Did the president really have that much unchecked power?

Critics went on the attack, arguing that the president's actions threatened the separation of powers, rule of law, the Constitution, and the system of checks and balances. And while George Bush was not the first president to move beyond the law, his bold assertion that the rule of law did not bind a president in times of war did mark a new and, critics charged, dangerous approach. It was a grave challenge to the Constitution and the separation of powers, as well as an extreme claim of presidential authority. At stake was no less than the integrity of the system of checks and balances. Battle lines were drawn. The president dug in his heels and his critics did likewise. Serious questions of constitutionalism were at stake.[10]

The Administration Defends the President's Prerogative Power

Initially, the 9/11 tragedy created conditions in which a public defense of the imperial presidency was hardly necessary. The president was handed a virtual "blank check," and no one—certainly not Congress—was required to endorse power over the executive. Necessity, emergency, and crisis brought to life a "prerogative presidency." But over time the president's critics questioned Bush's unilateral use of executive power.

Initially caught off guard, the administration did a fumbling job of publicly justifying its power grab. At first, it did not feel it needed to justify its actions. However, relying on "I'm a war president" had only so much staying power, and as the public demanded a more credible defense of the imperial presidency, the administration was caught with its intellectual pants down. It had to scramble to cull together a defense of the president's claims of imperial power.

President Bush was comfortable exercising a swaggering style of leadership that was dubbed "the Un-Hidden Hand." There was nothing subtle about this ostentatious approach.[11] It was leadership by sledgehammer. For a time, it worked. Yet in the end, boldness proved insufficient. What were the constitutional underpinnings of such presidential boldness?[12]

The Origins of the Unitary Executive Theory

The accumulation of all powers, legislative, executive, and judiciary, in the same hands, whether of one, a few, or many, and whether hereditary, self-appointed, or elective, may justly be pronounced the very definition of tyranny.

—James Madison, *The Federalist Papers*, No. 47

The origins of the Bush administration's expansive view of presidential power can be seen in what is called the *unitary executive*.[13] The unitary executive represents a new challenge to the rule of law. While the administration rarely provided a comprehensive defense of its actions, we can nonetheless make the arguments the administration *should* have made in defense of its expansive use of presidential power and thereby put these ideas to the "smell test."

The unitary executive may be seen as consisting of seven elements:[14]

1. executive prerogative, based on John Locke's *Second Treatise*
2. "energy" in the executive, grounded in Alexander Hamilton's defense of presidential authority
3. the "coordinate constitution" view of the Constitution, where the "executive power" is fused with the "commander-in-chief" clause
4. the doctrine of "necessity," as practiced, for example, by Abraham Lincoln during the Civil War
5. selected supporting court decisions
6. the "constitutional dictatorship," as described by Clinton Rossiter
7. precedent and past practices of US presidents

John Locke's "Executive Prerogative"

When, if ever, is a president justified in going beyond the law and violating the Constitution? Although the word *emergency* does not appear in the Constitution, nor did the framers include any provision for extraconstitutional crisis leadership (though there was ample historical precedent from other governments they might well have included), some scholars believe that the founders did envision the possibility of a president exercising "supraconstitutional powers" in a time of national emergency.[15]

Historically, though not constitutionally, during a crisis, the president assumes extraconstitutional powers.[16] The president's institutional position offers a unique vantage point from which to exert strong crisis leadership, and Congress, the courts, and the public usually accept the president's judgments and power grabs. This pedigree can be traced back to philosopher John Locke.[17] To Locke, no law could anticipate every eventuality. Therefore, Locke argued that under extraordinary circumstances the government—the executive—could on occasion go against written law in order to handle a crisis. This is referred to as prerogative. Yet no such Lockean prerogative found its way into the Constitution, and virtually all evidence from the founding era suggests that the inventors of the presidency *rejected* such prerogative powers.

Alexander Hamilton's Call for "Energy" in the Executive

While most scholars of the presidency and the Constitution conclude that the framers invented an executive of *limited authority* grounded in a *separation and sharing of power* under the *rule of law*,[18] some modern executive-power advocates (presidentialists) bypass the bulk of the historical record and selectively choose to highlight only those bits of evidence that support their strong executive preference, ignoring the voluminous evidence to the contrary of their preferred view.[19] They often dismiss their critics without facing them, creating a convenient constitutional shroud for presidential power without doing the hard work of making the constitutional case for the robust presidency they so desire and making the separation of powers sing with a distinctly presidential voice.[20] Who among the framers is their one guiding light? Alexander Hamilton. Advocates of the Bush position claim Hamilton as an intellectual forefather.

Elements of Hamilton's case for an energetic presidency can be found in *Federalist*, no. 70. It reads in part:

> There is an idea, which is not without its advocates, that a vigorous executive is inconsistent with the genius of republican government. . . .
>
> Energy in the executive is a leading character in the definition of good government. It is essential to the protection of the community against foreign attacks: It is not less essential to the steady administration of the laws, to the protection of property against those irregular and high handed combinations, which sometimes interrupt the ordinary course of justice, to the security of liberty against the enterprises and assaults of ambition, of faction and of anarchy. . . .
>
> A feeble executive implies a feeble execution of the government. A feeble execution is but another phrase for a bad execution: And a government ill executed, whatever it may be in theory, must be in practice a bad government. . . .
>
> Taking it for granted, therefore, that all men of sense will agree in the necessity of an energetic executive; it will only remain to inquire, what are the ingredients which constitute this energy. . . .
>
> The ingredients, which constitute energy in the executive, are first unity, secondly duration, thirdly an adequate provision for its support, fourthly competent powers.

But it must be pointed out that an energetic presidency is not necessarily an imperial presidency. And Hamilton's energetic executive is but a part of Hamilton's or the framers' story. Even Hamilton did not advocate so robust a presidency as the unitary executive advocates would like. Hamilton's energetic executive was always a *part* of a republican order, not a unilateralist one. Taken in its totality, the evidence that emerges from a thorough examination of his writings, especially in *The Federalist Papers*, reveals a more circumscribed presidency than the Bush advocates suggest.

Coordinate Construction of the Constitution

By combining two provisions in the Constitution, the executive-power ("vesting") clause and the commander-in-chief clause (both in Article II), advocates of the unitary executive theory see a geometric expansion of executive authority, where the parts, added together, multiply in significance, creating a plenary authority for the president. Conveniently forgotten is the fact that the president also takes an oath to "take Care that the Laws be faithfully executed," even the laws with which he may personally disagree.[21] This is designed to bind the president to the rule of law.[22]

Some Bush administration officials see presidential authority in times of war as creating an executive of virtually unchecked power. A September 25, 2002, Office of Legal Counsel (OLC) memo argues that "these decisions [in wartime] under our Constitution are for the President alone to make."[23] Other OLC memos suggest that the president may do things that are unlawful and that neither Congress nor the courts have the authority to review presidential acts in a time of war.[24] However, this expansive reading of the Constitution violates both the spirit and the letter of the law. The Supreme Court, in cases such as *Hamdi v. Rumsfeld* (2004) and *Rasul v. Bush* (2004), and Congress, in efforts such as its ban on the use of torture (a bill President Bush signed but then argued in a "signing statement" that although he was signing the bill into law, he did not consider himself bound by the law he had just signed), have attempted to reclaim some of the power that was lost, delegated, ceded, or stolen.

The Doctrine of Necessity

Perhaps no claim by the Bush administration resonates as powerfully as the "necessity" argument. The old Roman adage *Inter arma silent leges* (In war, the laws are silent), though not constitutionally valid, still holds persuasive political power.[25] Abraham Lincoln relied on the doctrine of necessity during the Civil War, arguing to Congress on July 4, 1861:

> The attention of the country has been called to the proposition that one who is sworn to "take care that the laws be faithfully executed," should not himself violate them. Of course some consideration was given to the questions of power, and propriety, before this matter was acted upon. . . . To state the question more directly, are all the laws, *but one*, to go unexecuted, and the government itself go to pieces, lest that one be violated? Even in such a case, would not the official oath be broken, if the government should be overthrown, when it was believed that disregarding the single law would tend to preserve it?

Lincoln believed that it was the Union (nation) that had to be preserved, because without the Union, the Constitution and the rule of law were meaningless.[26] In short, the Constitution *was not* a suicide pact.[27] In an 1864 letter to Senator Albert Hodges, Lincoln gives his rationale for the exercise of this extraordinary presidential power, writing:

> I have never understood that the Presidency conferred upon me an unrestricted right to act officially upon this [his own] judg-

ment and feeling. It was in the oath I took that I would, to the best of my ability, preserve, protect, and defend the Constitution of the United States. . . . I did understand however, that my oath to preserve the Constitution to the best of my ability imposed upon me the duty of preserving, by every indispensable means, that government—that nation—of which that Constitution was the organic law. Was it possible to lose the nation, and yet preserve the Constitution? . . . I felt that measures, otherwise unconstitutional, might become lawful, by becoming indispensable to the preservation of the Constitution, through the preservation of the nation.

Had the Bush administration relied on the necessity argument, they would have been on powerful (if unconstitutional) ground. For some reason, they chose to go further. They claimed that not only was it necessary to go beyond the law but that in such cases, violating the law is not "really" violating the law. They are, they argued, *above the law* in times of war.[28] The Bush administration claimed a legal basis for the monarchical presidency. And although the evidence of such a legal footing is virtually nonexistent, this assertion, matched by bold action, meeting little congressional opposition, became practice and perhaps precedent. A claim of Nixonian proportions, it literally does away with law and replaces it with the will of the executive. To go back to President Nixon:

> *Nixon:* Well, when the president does it, that means that it is not illegal.
> *Frost:* By definition.
> *Nixon:* Exactly. Exactly. If the president determines that a specified action is necessary to protect national security, then the action is lawful, even if it is prohibited by a federal statute.[29]

While the Supreme Court sought on several occasions to delegitimize these monarchical pretensions,[30] the Bush administration continued to press its case, largely ignoring the will of the Court. The Justice Department's Office of Legal Counsel memos attempted to place a legal fig leaf over bold claims of power, yet most were mere assertions of power with little supporting evidence.[31] These memos, combined with the president's view on "signing statements" (that he could sign a bill into law yet claim that he need not follow the law just signed),[32] lead to a president above the law because *he is* the law.

This is precisely the executive the framers sought to neuter under the rule of law and separation of powers. As Justice Robert Jackson wrote in *Youngstown*, "The prerogative exercised by George III, and the description of its evils in the Declaration of Independence," left no doubt "that the framers stripped the new president of kingly prerogative." President Lincoln never made such audacious claims. Even as he went beyond the letter of the law, he never claimed an inherent authority to breach the law, and he always recognized that Congress had the ultimate authority to reject his claims of power. If Lincoln momentarily went beyond the law—out of necessity—it was still the law and not his will that was to be supreme. It is this distinction that separates the Bush version of presidential power from its predecessors.

Likewise, President Franklin D. Roosevelt, in the early stages of the Great Depression, confronted the crisis by admitting that some of his actions might go beyond the literal scope of the law. In his March 4, 1933, inaugural address, Roosevelt called for increased presidential power:

> It is to be hoped that the normal balance of executive and legislative authority may be wholly adequate to meet the unprecedented task before us. But it may be that an unprecedented demand and need for undelayed action may call for temporary departure from

that normal balance of public procedure. . . . [I]n the event that the national emergency is still critical, I shall not evade the clear course of duty that will then confront me. I shall ask the Congress for the one remaining instrument to meet the crisis, broad Executive power to wage a war against the emergency, as great as the power that would be given to me if we were in fact invaded by a foreign foe.

Selected Supportive Supreme Court Decisions

In general, the courts have not served as a very effective check on presidential power.[33] Although there have been times when the courts tried to stand up to the president (e.g., in some of the Civil War cases, early in the New Deal era, late in the Watergate period, and late in the war against terrorism), overall, the courts have shied away from direct confrontations with presidents and have quite often been willing to defer to or add to the powers of the presidency.

Presidentialists gravitate toward one court case in particular, *United States v. Curtiss-Wright Export Corp.* (1936). In that case, Justice George Sutherland drew on a speech delivered in the House of Representatives in 1800 by then member of Congress and later Supreme Court Chief Justice John Marshall, who referred to the president as "the sole organ" of American foreign policy. This reference found its way into Sutherland's opinion and became a rallying cry for modern-day presidentialists. While Sutherland's "sole organ" remark was merely a judicial aside (dicta), it became the unofficial executive-branch mantra for any president's bold assertion of broad and unregulated power over foreign affairs. Scholars have found little in *Curtiss-Wright* to rely on in the defense of the prerogative presidency, and other than to defenders of presidential power, this case is not seen as significant in granting presidents expansive powers.[34] Interestingly, presidentialists rarely cite the number of cases that limit the president's imperial authority.

Clinton Rossiter and the Constitutional Dictatorship

Scholar Clinton Rossiter's "constitutional dictatorship" is an effort to come to grips with the problem Locke and other democratic theorists attempted to solve.[35] The "constitutional dictatorship" is a stark admission of the failure of democratic theory to come to terms with emergencies. Nowhere in the Constitution is it specified that the president should have additional powers in times of crisis. Yet history gives us ample precedents where in times of crisis, the powers of the president have increased.[36]

Under Rossiter's theory, democracies cannot handle the demands of crisis and must invest additional powers in the executive. The Court and Congress recognize the emergency and allow the president to employ additional powers. But to be legitimate, the constitutional dictator must also recognize the limits of his powers. Franklin D. Roosevelt, in 1942, after requesting that Congress grant him an unusually large amount of power, assured the legislature that "when the war is won, the powers under which I act automatically revert to the people—to whom they belong."[37] The executive, in short, must return the extraordinary powers it has grabbed during the crisis to their rightful place. Yet questions remain as to (1) whether presidents have returned these powers and (2) whether, even if the president desired to do so, a complete return to normality is possible after dictatorial or quasi-dictatorial power is placed in the hands of one man.

The Weight of Precedent

Advocates of the unitary executive argue that there are sufficient precedents to justify President Bush's activities. Lincoln during the

Civil War, Woodrow Wilson in World War I, FDR during the Depression and World War II, and others paved the path that Bush followed. Yet so did Richard Nixon, and while his actions are almost universally condemned, his "When the president does it that means it is not illegal" motto was clearly embraced by the Bush administration.[38]

Precedent is a useful but uncertain guide in the war against terrorism. After all, this is, by President Bush's own admission, a war without an end. Even if one were tempted to give presidents some leverage in this, a permanent prerogative presidency would do such constitutional violence to the American system as to force the abandonment of constitutional government in favor of something more closely resembling the one-man rule the framers so vehemently rejected. In this case, the United States would have come full circle from a revolution against the executive tyranny of the king of England to the embrace of imperial rule in the modern era.

The Unitary Executive and Crisis Government

The predicate to an expansive presidency is, first of all, a legitimate and widely recognized crisis. Only in a genuine emergency can a president exercise extraconstitutional power. Also, the other branches and the public must be willing to cede these powers to the president. Third, the president must ultimately be willing to bow to the will of Congress if it chooses to set policy or limit the president's exercise of power. And the president cannot use secrecy and distortion to hide from congressional or public scrutiny. In general, Lincoln and FDR followed these guidelines; Nixon did not. And what of George W. Bush in the post-9/11 era? Bush had the predicate, but he was reluctant to place himself within the rule of law. He exercised extraconstitutional power *and* claimed that his acts were not reviewable by Congress or the courts, often cloaking his actions in secrecy and duplicity.[39] Such a bold interpretation of the president's prerogative powers is not supported by law or history.

The Bush administration took the unitary executive further than its predecessors, claiming that in war, the president's actions are "nonreviewable."[40] Thus, the Bush administration asserted a plenary presidency that was above the law, above the Constitution, and unbound by the separation of powers, rule of law, and checks and balances. In this, the Bush defense would add a seventh pillar to the unitary executive: no other branch may question our actions.

It must be remembered that the framers rejected Locke's prerogative in favor of checks and balances, they rejected Hamilton's expansive executive for Madisonian equilibrium, and while "necessity" is a powerful political argument, it is not a persuasive constitutional argument. Modern-day presidentialists, leapfrog backward, largely ignoring the work of the framers, preferring instead to go back to the very British precedents our framers rejected. As John Yoo writes, "In interpreting the meaning of the Declare War Clause, we should not look exclusively at what a particularly influential Framer said about the provision at the Federal Convention. To better understand historical context, we should look to the British Constitution." In *War by Other Means*, Yoo openly reveals his selective use of evidence, admitting, "I *decided* to take Hamilton as my role model."[41] *Decided* to take Hamilton? One does not decide what evidence to accept on the basis of personal preference but must rely on the full weight of *all* the evidence. If anyone should serve as a model of the Constitution, it is James Madison. Evidence, not choice, must guide judgment.[42]

In an age of terrorism, is the unitary executive, the monarchal presidency, or the imperial presidency a permanent fixture of our political system?[43] Or can we strike the right balance between the needs of security and the demands of the rule of law? We need a presidency that is both powerful and accountable, robust yet under the rule of law. But how to achieve these worthy ends? Our answers to these questions will shape the nation for the coming generation and determine whether the experiment in self-government was a fool's game or the solution to our problems.

The Bush administration's efforts to condense the three branches into one (executive) is not the answer. Rejecting constitutionalism in favor of executive autocracy may sound appealing, but it gives the terrorists far too much. Why so willingly cede to al-Qaeda the integrity of our constitutional system? It is a victory they have neither earned nor deserve.

Debating Presidential Power

The ongoing debate between the *presidentialists* and the *constitutionalists* often occurs at the extreme ends of polar positions.[44] Each camp digs in its heels and concedes little to its adversary. A more interesting case for presidential supremacy is made by Posner and Vermeule. Unlike Yoo, who argues that the president's imperial powers are constitutionally grounded, Posner and Vermeule see a Madisonian presidency, created by the framers, as limited and weak. The presidency was intended to be a weak office because the framers had a deep fear of executive tyranny, what Posner and Vermeule call "tyrannophobia."[45] So they enchained the presidency in a web of both legal (the Constitution) and political (separation of powers) restraints. The framers *wanted* the president to be relatively weak.

But historical developments and the war against terror require, they argue, a more powerful, more centralized presidency. Posner and Vermeule see this more powerful presidency developing over time, and they approve of this transformation. In essence, they argue, the presidency has outgrown the Constitution, and we should both recognize and welcome that development. "There is," they argue, "no pragmatically feasible alternative to executive government under current conditions." They further argue, "The executive—alone of national institutions—has the capacity to take action in the real world, outside of law books, and that action changes the status quo facing other institutions. Where it is more difficult for those institutions to undo the new status quo the executive has set than it would have been to block the change initially, the power of unilateral de facto action becomes highly consequential." This does not condone the imperial presidency—at least not the imperial presidency social scientists usually describe: "Does the president himself, then, possess imperial power? Not in the overheated sense in which liberal historians and political scientists refer to the 'imperial presidency.' Liberal legalists equate the absence of effective *legal* constraints on the executive with the absence of *any* constraints, yet even an imperial president is constrained by politics and public opinion. Most fundamental is the reelection constraint." And they conclude that "political constraints on executive government are real, even as legal constraints have atrophied." The key to preventing executive tyranny, to Posner and Vermeule, can be found not in the web of laws, but in the constraints of democratic politics. And so "the Madisonian separation of powers is obsolete." What comes after Madison is "a new political order in which government is centered on the executive."[46]

The constitutionalists, on the other hand, see the president as enchained in a Madisonian system of checks and balances within a separation-of-powers system. This system was intentionally designed by the framers to limit presidential powers. As Harold Hongju Koh notes, this design was meant to elicit a form of power sharing by the president and Congress, both of whom had a significant role in making policy.[47] Unlike Posner and Vermeule, who also acknowledge that the framers established a circumscribed presidency but that such a presidency is no longer viable or desirable, Koh points out the positive elements of the framers' power-sharing model. (See Table 5.1 for a review of various positions.)

TABLE 5.1 Evolving Interpretations of the President's War/Emergency Powers

	Presidential Supremacists	Political Constitutionalists	Constitutionalists
Who:	John Yoo Eric Posner and Adrian Vermeule	Thomas Cronin/ Michael Genovese Andrew Rudalevige	Harold Koh David Gray Adler
Power:	Expansive Independent of Congress	Shared	Narrow
Primary Authority:	President	President (with Congress)	Congress
Source:	Practice	Constitution/politics/ circumstances	Congress
Description:	Unitary executive	Political executive	Circumscribed executive
Goal:	Strength and security in a dangerous world	Sound policy in a dangerous world	Rule of law "chain the dog of war"
Model:	George W. Bush	George H. W. Bush	James Madison
Requirement:	Presidential decision/action	Presidential action/ Congressional approval	Congressional decision
Court Case:	Curtiss-Wright	Youngstown	Milligan
Power is:	Inherent/implied Article II	Inherent/implied/ delegated	Expressed Article II
Basis:	Necessity/function structure	Combination	Rule of law Constitution Will of Congress
Nutshell:	Imperial presidency on steroids	Presidential leadership	President must gain consent of Congress

Koh, here writing about the nation's foreign policy powers, sees the Constitution setting up a system that

> rests upon a simple notion: that generally speaking, the foreign af-
> fairs power of the United States is a *power shared* among the three
> branches of the national government. . . . In foreign as well as do-
> mestic affairs, the Constitution requires that we be governed by
> separated institutions *sharing* foreign policy powers. Under this
> constitutional power-sharing scheme, the president, Congress, and
> the courts all play integral roles in both making and validating
> foreign-policy decisions. As it has evolved, the National Security
> Constitution assigns to the president the predominant role in that
> process, but affords him only a limited realm of exclusive powers
> with regard to diplomatic relations and negotiations and to the
> recognition of nations and governments. Outside of that realm,
> governmental decisions regarding foreign affairs must transpire
> within a sphere of concurrent authority, under presidential man-
> agement, but bounded by the checks provided by congressional
> consultation and judicial review. In short, the structural principle
> that animates our National Security Constitution is *balanced in-
> stitutional participation.*[48]

Between the supremacists and the constitutionalists can be found the *political constitutionalists.*[49] Those who espouse this position see the Constitution as creating a shared model of power that circum-scribes the presidency, and like most observers (John Yoo being one of the few exceptions) acknowledge that this Madisonian model stems from the framers' concerns that the executive could become tyrannical.

Where those who hold this view break from the constitutional-ists is in their greater willingness to cede the necessity argument to the supremacists. Yet the political constitutionalists do not embrace the supremacists' description of the president's constitutional power, nor do they (we) accept their prescription: a powerful (and largely unfettered) presidency. Rather, they see strong *and* constitutional leadership as the goal. The president is not the errand boy of the legislature, nor is the office to be expansively understood. It is a significant leadership institution, and it is at its best when it can build coalitions, reach consensus, and bring Congress into the decision-making process.

Political scientist Andrew Rudalevige notes the need for *both* Congress and the president to be assertive. He writes, "All presidents try to push the limits of their power: it is inherent in the office's position in the constitutional framework. The key question becomes, then, 'Will other political actors push back?'"[50]

Conclusion

This chapter has argued that we are in a new and constitutionally dangerous era. The notions of limited constitutional government, the rule of law, separation of powers, and checks and balances are being frontally assaulted by those who argue either that the framers did not intend to limit presidential power but to unleash it or that they did intend to limit the executive but that today such a notion is "obsolete."

In this we have come full circle from a direct rejection of monarchical prerogative to an embrace of such powers. It need not be this way. We can create a presidency that is both powerful and accountable. The presidency has thus become our "most dangerous branch of government." We turn next to our cures.

6

A Cure for the Imperial Presidency

If (a) the United States was established as a constitutional republic, yet (b) we have become a presidential nation, should we (c) reclaim our place as a constitutional republic by cutting down to size the scope of presidential power or (d) admit that the twenty-first century requires strong presidential leadership and redesign our system to reflect the demands of modernization?

I will agree that as much as we may wish to go back to the original design and distribution of power in the framers' Constitution, this could happen only if we retreat from global leadership and drastically reduce the size and scope of the federal government. This is unlikely to happen.[1] I will further argue that in maintaining the fiction that we are still a constitutional republic, bounded by the Constitution of 1787, we are living a lie that does damage to the rule of law. We must open our eyes and admit that in practice we are no longer a constitutional republic but a presidential nation. Further, I argue that we must reclaim the rule of law and constitutionalism by admitting that we need a strong president but one under a regime of democratic accountability and a more streamlined separation-of-powers system that gives the president more legal power yet binds the office in a rejuvenated check-and-balance regime. In doing this, we can again claim to be guided by constitutional principle, but principles that better suit a modern superpower.

The system of checks and balances works best when presidential leadership animates and drives the system. But we are not here referring to just any type of presidential leadership. At his or her best, the president can be a leader, a teacher, a guide, and a mobilizer. Yet we must never forget that the office that nourishes responsible leadership is also capable of great abuse. In this, the presidency is necessary, yet always potentially dangerous. We cannot live without presidential power, yet living with it threatens constitutionalism and our traditional notions of the rule of law in a constitutional republic. How do we resolve this dilemma? How do we (a) transform our eighteenth-century Constitution into a twenty-first-century document designed for a world superpower and (b) support presidential power and leadership while we also (c) control and constitutionalize it? Can the presidency be made both powerful *and* accountable? In this we can be guided by the model presented by Clinton Rossiter more than a half century ago: "A strong president is a bad President, a curse upon the land, unless his means are constitutional and his ends democratic, unless he acts in ways that are fair, dignified, and familiar, and pursues policies to which a 'persistent and undoubted' majority of the people has given support. We honor the great Presidents of the past, not for their strength, but for the fact that they used it wisely to build a better America." Our goal, as Arthur M. Schlesinger Jr. reminds us in his book *The Imperial Presidency*, is to "devise means of reconciling a strong and purposeful Presidency with equally strong and purposeful forms of democratic control." He goes on to argue that we do need a strong president, but "one within the Constitution."[2]

The framers established separate institutions that shared powers as "the essential precaution in favor of liberty."[3] Ours is a three-branch system of government, and no single branch can eclipse the others in power to avoid the checks and balances of our system of governing. How, then, do we reinvigorate the system of powers for a modern age?

What is our goal reforming the presidency? I base my answer on several assumptions:

1. While the Congress is granted greater constitutional power than the presidency, Congress is not structured to lead—especially in the modern age. Thus, we *need strong presidential leadership* (or an "energetic executive).
2. But strong presidents can become tyrants. Thus, we *need strong agents of accountability.*
3. To do this, we must change Congress, the presidency, the Court, and the public.
4. This won't be easy.

What is the purpose of reform?[4] To bring our constitutional checks and balances into the twenty-first century. What are the problems we address? Power aggrandizement by presidents, lack of structures needed (and political spine) by Congress to responsibly confront presidents, failure to bring the Court into the process, and inflated and unrealistic demands and expectations by the public. How feasible are these reforms? Frankly, not very—at least not at present. But as we become more and more dissatisfied with govern- ment in general and the presidency in particular, these reform pro- posals could gain traction. What are the implications of these reforms? They are designed to constitutionally strengthen the presidency, structurally streamline the Congress, give the Court greater involvement, and make the public more realistic about what it can expect from government and the presidency. Will the benefits of these reforms outweigh the costs? Although there are always unintended consequences of reform, we have little choice but to attempt to revive the spirit of constitutionalism in America, lest we succumb to the false promise of a presidential savior-tyrant. How might these changes inform our conception of presidential leadership and American government? Perhaps we can breathe new life into the check-and-balance system, promote new respect for the rule of law, and create a more amicable process of governing. Finally, are these reforms designed to achieve "my" political and ideological preferences,[5] or are they truly for the benefit of the system as a whole? I leave you to answer that.

The Path to Reform

What is the scope of reform, major surgery or minor tinkering? Major surgery is politically unfeasible, and tinkering would not efficiently address the size of our problems. Those advocating major surgery often look to the British Westminster model of parliamentary democracy as their cure. While it is plausible that a parliamentary system (fusion of power) is preferable to a separation-of-powers system, the chances of the United States adopting such a system are so remote as to dissuade us from further comments on this possibility.[6]

At what level should we direct our reform agenda: the *individual*, the *institution*, or the *system*? There are those who lament the lack of insight, judgment, experience, and skills of our presidents, arguing that "if only we could find another FDR. . . ." Of course, better presidents would make the presidency better, but even a modern-day FDR would have difficulty governing our leaky ship of state.

Yes, we must also be aware that while the president is one person, the presidency is an *institution*. How do we give the president the institutional support he or she needs to make good decisions? And even with good support, decision making comes down to one person deciding. Would better information have changed George W. Bush in his desire to overthrow Saddam Hussein? Rockman notes this problem when he writes, "The problem of constitution-makers is to try to turn offices into institutions. That aspiration always is imperfectly met. Despite the apparatus that has grown around it, the American presidency today is more an office than an institution. For the most part, it is a fairly straightforward extension of the person who sits behind the desk in the Oval Office. In important decisions, cabinet officers often are ignored. Consultation is both *ad hoc* and *post hoc* but almost never institutionalized."[7]

Reforming the *system* often means the parliamentary panacea, yet as noted above, it is unlikely that the United States would import such a model to America. There are other systemic reforms that might be both attractive and attainable, however.

The Terrain of Reform

There is a wide range of reform options being suggested by others. Some focus on reducing the global role of the United States. Others focus on strengthening Congress or embracing the global role. Some advocate tinkering at the edges, but all are put forward as potential cures for the imbalance created by the move to a presidential nation.

A Return to Isolationism Versus Embracing Globalism

One suggestion, alluded to earlier, is to downsize the empire and downsize the emperor. If we truly wish to go back to the constitutional roots of the presidency—original intent—we must pull back from global leadership. A smaller global power can have a smaller presidency. Libertarian Gene Healy proposes just such a solution to our presidency problem, arguing that our adulation toward presidents creates a cult of the presidency that endangers republican government. And as a Libertarian, Healy calls for a ratcheting down of our public expectations of presidents, as well as a pulling back from our expensive commitments abroad. Even Harold Hongju Koh recognizes that "America's constitutionalism has grown increasingly incompatible with its globalism."[8]

On the other hand, others argue that if you want a constitutional presidency, go back to the original Constitution. Some modern conservatives, while still embracing a world leadership role for the United States, call for a stricter constitutionalism that downsizes the presidency.[9] The Libertarian cure is a dramatic downsizing of the presidency and the projections of American power abroad. The conservative cure is the same, only less so. Many conservatives call for a smaller presidency and smaller government, yet still cling to dreams of global leadership.

There are two schools of thought that argue that we can and must find a way to cope with the new demands of globalism. The conservative argument presented by John Yoo as well as Posner and Vermeule accepts the inevitability of a powerful presidency and asserts either that this powerful presidency was given to us by the framers (Yoo)[10] or that although not grounded in the Constitution, the Madisonian limited executive must, by *necessity*, give way to the powerful presidency (Posner and Vermeule).

A liberal variant on this sees a clash between the limited nature of the president's constitutional power and the demands of global leadership. Jules Lobel argues that we cannot have both constitutional fidelity and global leadership. Robert Spitzer shares these concerns and while recognizing that "liberalism and the American presidency are not necessarily a natural match" nonetheless sees a need for presidential activism and global leadership.[11]

A Strong Presidency Needs *a Strong Congress*

Some reformers, ceding that a strong presidency is necessary to preserve and promote US global leadership, seek to strengthen the check-and-balance system by calling also for a strong Congress, but not the Congress as currently structured. A stronger Congress that remains ill-suited to the modern capacity to move more quickly would only exacerbate the already debilitating deadlock that so often characterizes the congressional input to (non) policy making.

Thus, to revitalize Congress, we must streamline Congress, bringing it out of the eighteenth and into the twenty-first century. The presidency dominates because it can adapt. It can adapt because one hand is at the helm. As currently structured, Congress cannot govern, and it should not govern. If it wants to become relevant in an ongoing manner, Congress must become a modern institution, capable of providing accountability and timely decision making. Congress must streamline its process by giving greater authority to the Gang of 8, the top elected leaders from both parties. Today, a small number of activists in Congress can utterly tie up the entire institution, preventing it from conducting necessary business. By granting more authority to a Gang of 8, the leadership of Congress would be compelled to accept more responsibility and might be able to bypass the gridlock so often displayed in relations between the president and Congress.[12]

An Emergency Constitution

The framers did not put into the Constitution any provision for emergency transfers of power to the executive. They might have, as they were very familiar with republican Rome's constitution and its provisions under grave emergencies to temporarily turn dictatorial powers over to one man.

Yale's Bruce Ackerman proposes that the United States set up a system wherein during an emergency, a temporary dictatorship of sorts is created to deal with the crisis. This "emergency constitution" would be limited in duration and must meet a set of standards, but it would allow for the expansive use of power while not forcing the president to act beyond the law.[13]

Tinker While You Work

Those uncomfortable with the major-surgery option to reform often find the tinkering approach best suited to the needs of the times. Among the smaller reforms proposed we find:

One Six-Year Term: Some believe that the presidency is too political an office. And as politicians, presidents look to promote policies that will get themselves elected, even if they are not good for the country. Such critics argue that by limiting the president to one six-year term, we could take politics out of the office. Could we? Should we?

Proponents claim that the single six-year term might remove a president from some of the more negative kind of partisan politics, the assumption being that once elected to a six-year term, with no possibility of reelection, presidents might eschew partisan calculations and provide leadership for all of the people. Thus, presidents might become more inclined to do what is right even if this meant their party would lose votes or their own political future might be damaged. Former Lyndon Johnson aide Jack Valenti wrote that "if the Watergate mess tells us anything it is that the reelection of a President is the most nagging concern in the White House." Further, he asserted that "Watergate would never have occurred if Presidential aides were not obsessed with reelection. If they had been comfortable in tenure, knowing that in six years they would lose their lease—and in that short time they must write their record as bravely and wisely as possible—is it not possible that their arrogance might have softened and their reach for power might have shortened?"[14]

Despite some attractive features, the six-year term would probably cause more problems than it would solve. The required reelection after four years is one of the more democratic aspects of the presidency. It gives citizens an opportunity for assessment and enhances the likelihood that a president will weigh the effects of whatever he does on his reelection chances. Moreover, a political party should retain the threat of dumping a president as a check on the incumbent and the office, especially on a president who refuses to honor his party's pledges.

When in 1913 the US Senate passed a resolution in favor of the single six-year term, Woodrow Wilson argued against it. His reasoning is still valid: "The argument is not that it is clearly known now just how long each President should remain in office. Four years is too long a term for a President who is not the true spokesman of the people, who is imposed upon and does not lead. It is too short a term for a President who is doing, or attempting, a great work of reform, and who has not had time to finish it." Wilson also contended that "to change the term to six years would be to increase the likelihood of its being too long without any assurance that it would, in happy cases, be long enough. A fixed constitutional limitation to a single term of office is highly arbitrary and unsatisfactory from any point of view."[15]

The proposed divorce between the presidency and politics presupposes a different kind of political system from the one we have. Our system is glued together largely by compromise and the extensive sharing of powers. In light of the requisites of democracy, the presidency should be a highly political office and the president an expert practitioner of the art of politics. There is no other way for presidents to build coalitions. A president who remains aloof from politics, campaigns, and partisan alliances does so at the risk of becoming a prisoner of events, special interests, or his own hubris.

The key means of bringing a president in touch with reality is the process of political debate, compromise, and bargaining, with all of their uncertainty, changes of course, arguments, and listening to different points of view. Domestic politics is full of groups to persuade and committees to inform, a quality that makes it distasteful to presidents but is, in fact, one of its virtues. Indeed, it is a source of hope we have for maintaining an open presidency, one that is not bound by its own sources of information and not too proud to still listen to others.

Most of our effective presidents have been highly political. They knew how to stretch the limited resources of the office. They loved politics and enjoyed the responsibilities of party leadership. Overall, the nation has been well served by sensitive politicians disciplined by party and public opinion. Many of our least-political presidents were also the least effective and seemingly the least suited temperamentally to the rigors of the office.

Today, everything a president does has political consequences, and every political act by a president has implications for the state of the presidency. We must recognize that presidents will and must be political and that they ought to be partisan leaders. Bipartisanship has often been overrated. James MacGregor Burns aptly noted that "almost as many crimes have been committed in the name of mindless bipartisanship as in the name of mindless patriotism."[16]

President's Question Time: In order to make presidents more accountable and answerable for their actions, some call for a "presidential question time." Similar to the prime minister's question time in England, the president would periodically appear before Congress and answer its questions. Those who favor such an idea argue that it would encourage transparency and help elevate the debate over an administration's policies. It could be done without a constitutional amendment and could even be done as an experiment for a year or two. A US version might take place once a month and therefore not place unreasonable demands on a president's time. A president already has to prepare for similar give-and-take exchanges with the press, so why not hold similar dialogues with Congress?

Critics point out that our system of separate branches differs from a parliamentary system, and this proposal might confuse that separation. Also, presidential cabinet members as well as top military and intelligence officers already participate in congressional committee hearings. Often, these administration officials are as well, if not better, informed on detailed policy matters than are most presidents. In addition, presidents regularly meet with party leaders—both their own and those of the opposition—at the White House, and these exchanges are likely to be more productive than the theater of a "president's question time."

This reform would also be questionable for political reasons. Presidents are unlikely to risk their independence and lessen the clout of their "bully pulpit" by submitting to what could be heated and acrimonious cross-examinations by opposition party leaders. Presidents are unlikely to give their opponents such a prominent forum.

A No-Confidence Option: When a British prime minister faces significant criticism, he or she may be politically vulnerable and Parliament may vote "no confidence" in the prime minister. With a successful no-confidence vote, the prime minister is removed from office, the Parliament is dissolved, and new national elections are held.

Sixteen states currently have recall provisions in their constitutions. Why not do the same for presidents? How might a no-confidence amendment work? A two-thirds vote of the members of each House present and voting would be necessary. Such a resolution would take priority over any other pending issue before Congress. If adopted, Congress would fix a date, between ninety and one hundred days, for a special election for the president and vice president as well as members of Congress. If it occurs near the regular congressional election date, that date could be used. The incumbent president is eligible to stand for reelection even though he or she was the target of the no-confidence vote.

Proponents of the no-confidence or national recall proposals believe the four-year fixed term is sometimes a liability when we have incompetent or corrupt presidents who lose the confidence of the nation. Incompetence, they point out, is not an impeachable offense. A "no-confidence" vote might also be a way to reconstitute a failed administration.

A goal of the proposed vote of no confidence is to make future presidents more accountable to Congress, as well as to the American people. But in many ways the president is already accountable to Congress, some say too much so. Because Congress often fails to do its constitutional job of keeping presidents accountable does not mean that the power is missing; it may be that they lack the political will to stand up to a president.

A vote of no confidence might lead presidents to avoid making controversial changes in policy that would antagonize key members of Congress. Innovative leadership might be thwarted, as presidents gear most of their actions to public opinion polls or to the wishes of the majority at the expense of minority rights or sound policy. This proposal might lead a president to concentrate on short-term popular initiatives to "create" favorable public approval at the expense of long-term planning.

Repeal the Twenty-Second Amendment: After the presidency of Franklin D. Roosevelt, a Republican-led effort to limit presidents to no more than two terms became law when the Twenty-Second

Amendment passed in 1951. Advocates of repeal argue that the two-term limit violates American citizens' right to decide who their leader will be. If the people want to vote for someone, especially an experienced veteran in the White House, there should be no rule telling them they do not have that right.

Every president's sun begins to set the day the second term begins, part of what is called the "lame duck" syndrome. We have, some say, dealt the presidency a severe blow by depriving second-term presidents of the political weapon that the possibility of another term gives them—the ability to keep both supporters and rivals guessing. Advocates of a strong presidency fear that the Twenty-Second Amendment limitation weakens presidential independence and weights the balance of power too much in the direction of Congress—a branch they fear is too unwieldy, risk averse, and "leaky" to provide strong leadership in the twenty-first century.

Proponents of retaining the Twenty-Second Amendment say eight years is more than enough time for a president to achieve his key goals. The notion of rotation in office, they argue, is healthy and desirable, especially in a robust constitutional democracy.

Reform the War Powers: The Constitution is clear: only Congress has the power to declare war. Yet over time presidents have ignored the Constitution and on numerous occasions ordered American troops into combat. In the modern world, where the United States serves as the only superpower, can the war power be tamed and brought back under congressional control? Given the importance of the decision to go to war, it seems vital to put presidential decisions under closer scrutiny and tighter congressional controls.

Of course, Congress *already has* all the constitutional authority it needs to tame the presidency in war. What is lacking is the political will. When presidents grab the war powers, Congress meekly retreats. Where presidents act, Congress hesitates. Strengthening the

War Powers Resolution might help, but there is no constitutional or statutory way to instill more institutional or personal backbone into Congress. If Congress wishes to "chain the dog of war," it already has all the necessary tools. The problem is that these tools are rusting away from disuse.

The Impeachment Option: No US president has ever been impeached and convicted. Only two have been impeached. This leads some critics to lament that the impeachment process has no teeth. The bar is—and should be—high regarding impeachments. It is a blunt instrument and should be reserved only for the most grievous of "high crimes and misdemeanors." Yet as such, it plays little role in the ongoing accountability of the presidency.

An option short of impeachment discussed but not utilized during the Clinton impeachment effort was to censure the president. Though nowhere mentioned in the Constitution, censure is a means—short of impeachment—of declaring acts of a president to be unacceptable. Congress censured Andrew Jackson (though it was later rescinded), and there is no reason it could not revive this practice. There is no formal penalty attached to *censure*, yet it might be a significant embarrassment and slap on the wrist to a president on the receiving end.

My Immodest Proposal(s)

The presidency is broken, and it needs to be fixed. But it is not *so* broken that we need to perform major surgery. How can we (1) empower the president to govern on a global stage, (2) ensure accountability, and (3) protect the rights and liberties so valued by Americans? Reforming the presidency is not enough. We must take an integrated or holistic approach to reform. Herewith, my immodest proposal:

1. The President and the Presidency: The most important quality in a president is good judgment.[17] Yet there are a variety of decision-making traps into which we often fall. What quality of mind is most likely to lead to good judgment?

In Japanese, *shin-kan* means "true sword." In modern understanding, we might define it as to do something truly, correctly, with purpose, and with success. Aristotle, in his *Nichomachean Ethics*, tried to guide the statesperson toward effective leadership in his discussion of *phronesis*. *Phronesis* means "knowledge put into appropriate action for a good cause." It is reason and good judgment, sound logic as applied to a complex world, recognizing the limits and possibilities at hand, and deciding on a constructive course of action that is most likely to lead to a morally and politically good result. Wisdom, prudence, good judgment, morally appropriate ends—these are the factors that bring *phronesis* to light. It is moral discernment applied to complex human affairs or prudence in action, goal maximization directed toward socially good ends, the effort to convert morally and socially sound ideals into policy—and it is what defines good presidential leadership. *Phronesis* goes beyond mere prudence; it is prudent judgment directed into action to achieve a good result. It is *judgment* and *action*.

Whom did Aristotle see as a leader with *phronesis*? Aristotle had his eye on the great Athenian statesman Pericles. To Aristotle, Pericles had the ability to see what was good and to translate that vision into policies designed to achieve those worthy and attainable goals (the Peloponnesian War notwithstanding). Pericles served the public interest even as he shaped it. He sought justice in an unjust world and had the skill and insight to translate his vision into policy. If you are looking for presidents who might fit this model, look to George Washington, Abraham Lincoln, and Franklin D. Roosevelt. In general, they did the right things for the right reasons, toward the right ends. Our presidents need to be schooled in the benefits of *phronesis*, and voters need to reward those who exhibit such qualities.

2. Congress: The real work of reforming the presidency takes place in Congress. Presently, Congress is just not doing its constitutional or political duty. The congressional process must be streamlined so that a president can more fruitfully consult with Congress. Presidential initiative must go to Congress *before* action is taken—even in covert operations—and Congress must establish a fast-track decision process to respond to a president in a timely fashion. The president must meet with the Gang of 8 on a regular basis, and this congressional leadership group must have the authority—if it deems it necessary—to postpone (for up to forty-eight hours) presidential acts while placing the president's plan before a fast-track congressional vote.

Harold Hongju Koh calls for the creation of a *core consultative group* in Congress. The benefits of such a group can be seen in its ability to bring Congress into the decision-making process *before*, not after, decisions are made and actions taken. As Koh writes: "By first creating a core group of members, with whom the president and his staff could meet regularly and consult on national security matters, Congress could provide the executive with the benefit of its deliberative judgments without demanding unacceptable sacrifices in flexibility, secrecy, or dispatch. . . . The group would have formal authority to invoke the War Powers Resolution even if the president chose not to do so; its legislative proposals would be accorded a special fast-track status in the legislative process."[18] Koh also calls for the creation of a *congressional legal advisory*, giving Congress greater access to executive branch information. And, of course, Congress must reclaim the war powers.

Congress must be reformed and restructured if it is not merely to play a passive role. Andrew Rudalevige writes, "The critical question, then, is straightforward: why had Congress been so acquiescent? The fact is that we have had an invisible Congress as much as an imperial president. Must of the expansion in presidential power has not been taken but given."[19] Congress will remain on the outside looking in if it does not reform itself. The presidency is built for speed; Congress is built for deliberation. Deliberate it must, but Congress must also find ways to decide more efficiently. Until it does, presidents will find ways to bypass or blow past the lethargic legislative branch.

3. The Court: Conflicts between the president and Congress are inevitable. At times they may even be healthy. But they can also be debilitating. Congress must establish a direct appeal process for the Supreme Court to adjudicate conflicts between the president and Congress that cannot be resolved politically. Remember, ours is a three-branch system, and getting the Court involved earlier might be a useful step in fostering political agreements between the president and Congress before the disputes get to the Court.

Bruce Ackerman sees the Court as an essential protector of the rule of law. In his emergency constitution the Court would serve as a "guardian" of constitutionalism and the rule of law. But as Harold Hongju Koh points out, "Congress cannot legislate judicial courage, any more than it can legislate executive self-restraint or congressional willpower."[20]

4. The Public: Americans are a patriotic people. Yet we know precious little about our government and our Constitution. A national teach-in on the Constitution is needed, as is greater civic education in our schools. As Justice Potter Stewart observed in the *Pentagon Papers* case, "The only effective restraint upon executive policy and power . . . may lie in an enlightened citizenry—in an informed and critical public opinion which alone can protect the values of a democratic government."[21]

If citizens do not insist on their government promoting and protecting their rights and liberties, the rule of law will be in jeopardy.

An informed, intelligent, public-minded citizenry is the most important bulwark against tyranny.

Conclusion

If we are to mainstream constitutional government and the rule of law, we must find ways to make our eighteenth-century Constitution serve the needs of a twenty-first-century superpower. We cannot go back. As the great philosopher Woody Allen once said: "We stand here today at a great crossroads. One fork leads to utter chaos and despair, the other to complete annihilation. Let us hope we have the wisdom to choose the right one."

7

Conclusion

JUDGING AMERICA'S REPUBLICAN EXPERIMENT

The impact of 9/11 and of the ever-changing terrorist threat gives more power to the imperial presidency and places the separation of power ordained by the Constitution under unprecedented and at times unbearable strain.

—Arthur M. Schlesinger Jr., *War and the American Presidency*

A state of war is not a blank check for the president. . . . [H]istory and common sense teach us that an unchecked system of detention carries the potential to become a means for oppression and abuse of others.

—Justice Sandra Day O'Connor, *Hamdi v. Rumsfeld* (2004)

Inventing the American presidency was an experiment in republican executive development. No such office had existed before. Few such offices operate today. How well—or poorly—did this experiment work out?

Initially, the American system of separation of powers worked reasonably well. As the United States was not, until the twentieth century, a world military or economic power, the United States did quite well with a limited executive. On occasions when crisis enveloped the state, presidents such as Abraham Lincoln, citing "necessity," could circumvent the restrictions of the system of checks and balances and centralize power under the hand of one man, the president. On such occasions when presidents went beyond the rule of law to exercise a brand of unilateral presidential prerogative,[1] they nonetheless were emphatic that for their actions to be legitimate, Congress had to give—even retroactively—its approval. Without such approval, the president's actions were constitutionally untenable.

All this began to change after World War II. First, President Harry Truman claimed independent constitutional authority to engage American troops in combat during the Korean War. Then, President Eisenhower and his successors used covert actions to assert American interests and unilateral presidential power abroad, all done in secret, all done in the name of national security. But during the 1960s and 1970s, things began to unravel. The (presidential) war in Vietnam went badly, the Church Committee exposed a series of CIA-presidential abuses of covert activities, Watergate challenged the constitutional order, and in a final "last gasp" of presidential unilateralism, disgraced former president Nixon asserted, "When the president does it, that means it is not illegal." This view, and the imperial presidency that went along with it, was soundly rejected.

In the 1980s, Ronald Reagan made a concerted effort to revive the imperial presidency, but was stopped cold when the crimes of the Iran-Contra scandal were exposed. The post–World War II presidency kept pushing the limits of power, and after a time, Congress, the courts, and the public pushed back.

After 9/11, the Bush administration, bolstered by crisis, reasserted an imperial version of presidential power in its embrace of a "unitary" theory of executive power. Whereas there was initially very little pushback against the administration, when the full parameters of this unilateralist version of power emerged, opposition grew.

If the presidency of the nineteenth century was at the periphery of power, the presidency of the twenty-first is at the central core. If the presidency of the nineteenth century largely was small and circumscribed, the presidency of the twenty-first century is big, powerful, and the leader of the Western coalition. It is a different presidency in a different world.

What kind of presidency is best suited for that world? Posner and Vermeule make a powerful case for the presidency of today as having outgrown its Madisonian roots.[2] Yet if the world has changed, if America's power and responsibilities across the globe have changed, and if the presidency has changed, the Constitution *has not*. Thus, in our embrace of an imperial (even if necessary) presidency, we do deep violence to our Constitution. Somehow we must reconcile this dilemma.

Presidential Power in a Dangerous World

The dangers we face from extremism and terrorism, climate change, pandemics, population shifts, and resource depletion require a searching reappraisal of our constitutional practices. And like the framers of 1787, we, too, need to ask: what kind of presidency do we want?

The powers of the presidency have—absent any constitutional changes—grown dramatically over the years. Without any formal articulation of the expanded presidency, presidents have merely stepped in, acted, and taken power. Historian Arthur M. Schlesinger Jr. writes that the modern presidency "has come to see itself in messianic terms as the appointed savior of a world whose unpredictable dangers call for a rapid and incessant deployment of men, arms, and decisions behind a wall of secrecy." He adds, "This seems hard to reconcile with the American Constitution."[3] Congress has often turned a blind eye as willing enabler of the demise of its own constitutional powers and at other times actively delegated its powers to the executive.

When the next crisis hits, and it shall, will we be ready? Will we know what roles the president, Congress, the Court, and the public should assume?

We are today as vulnerable as ever to one-man crisis rule, because we have not yet had a *national conversation*, a *deliberative debate* on the scope of the government's emergency power. If we do not decide ahead of the next crisis when cooler heads may not prevail, we will plunge once again into the vortex of the constitutional dictatorship. If *we* do not decide, *they* will, and for constitutional democracy and the rule of law, it may be too late. If we do not lay down a set of rules, we will be stuck on the sidelines, mere observers, hoping we have a Lincoln and not a Bush in the White House.

Crises present a particularly vexing challenge to constitutional democracies. In *The Federalist Papers*, No. 1, Alexander Hamilton presents this dilemma in a different yet related way:

It has been frequently remarked that it seems to have been reserved to the people of this country, by their conduct and example, to decide the important question, whether societies of men are really capable or not of establishing good government from reflection and choice, or whether they are forever destined to depend for their political constitutions on accident and force. If there be any truth in the remark, the crisis at which we are arrived may with propriety be regarded as the era in which that decision is to be made; and a wrong election of the part we shall act may, in this view deserve, to be considered as the general misfortune of mankind.

"Reflection and choice," or "accident and force." It was Hamilton's challenge to his age, it was a challenge echoed by Abraham Lincoln in the Gettysburg Address, and it is likewise our challenge today.

With More Power, More Accountability

Can the presidency be strong *and* constitutional? Strong enough to fulfill its constitutional duties yet accountable enough not to pose a threat to our republican values? If the United States is the imperial power, must we also have an imperial presidency? Sadly, in many ways, we seem to have come full circle, from a revolution against the absolute power of a monarch to a presidency that more closely resembles the king than a republican president. Has the imperial presidency become the norm?

As the central leadership agent of our Madisonian system, we need a creative and effective president. But to what ends? What passes for democracy today is democracy in name only. Big money drives the engine of government. Presidential autonomy presides over our system. But, as political commentator Michael Lind reminds us, "Presidential democracy is not democracy." He adds, "Americans must conclude that democracy does not mean voting for this or that elective monarch every four years and then leaving government to the monarch's couriers. Democracy means continuous negotiation among powerful and relatively autonomous legislators who represent diverse interests in society."[4]

We celebrate democracy and worship our Constitution as we allow our democracy to be purchased by the highest bidder and our Constitution to be hijacked by fear and empire. The war against terrorism is but the latest of many challenges to constitutional government. Only an educated and aroused citizenry committed to the principles of constitutionalism and the rule of law can protect the republic. If we have the best democracy that money can buy, we have no democracy. If we have a president above the law, we have no constitutional republic.

Our constitutional system *is* slow in operation. Indeed, we *may* need to give more constitutional and legal power to the presidency in the modern age. But we have allowed presidents—usually with the best intentions—to hijack the Constitution and make a shambles of the rule of law. Thus, we have the *worst* of both worlds: a powerful presidency above the law and a deteriorating system of accountability.

Bolster the presidency, yes, but bolster also the multiple agencies of democratic accountability. Accountability involves not only responsiveness to majority desires at election time but also taking the Constitution into account day by day. It also suggests a performance guided by integrity and character. Accountability implies as well that key decisions be explained to the people, allowing them the opportunity to appraise how well a president is handling the responsibilities of the job.

The United States needs a strong and democratically controlled presidency and strong citizenship. Political theorist Benjamin R. Barber notes the difficulty inherent in such a goal: "At the heart of democratic theory lies a profound dilemma that has afflicted democratic practice at least since the eighteenth century. Democracy requires both effective leadership and vigorous citizenship: yet the conditions and consequences of leadership often seem to undermine civic vigor. Although it cries for both, democracy must customarily make do either with strong leadership or with strong citizens. For the most part, depending on devices of representation in large-scale societies, democracy in the West has settled for strong leaders and correspondingly weak citizens."[5] James Madison's caution in *The Federalist Papers*, No. 51, speaks volumes to us today: "If men were angels, no government would be necessary. If angels were to govern man, neither external nor internal controls in government would be necessary. . . . A dependence on the people is, no doubt, the primary control on the government. But experience has taught mankind the necessity for auxiliary precautions."

Is the Presidency Safe for Democracy?

Given that the world remains a dangerous place, given that Congress moves slowly, given that the unity and structure of the executive dispose it to act quickly when necessary, we can expect to see presidents, when confronted by grave threats, assume and exercise prerogative and unilateral powers.

But all unilateral acts are not equal. The president may have no constitutional ground on which to act, yet act he must. Therefore, to exercise this power, he must step outside the law and employ extraconstitutional powers. This places a great deal on the shoulders of the president. Not only must he solve the problem, but he must also recognize that he has no strictly legal authority on which to act and must in the end place his actions before Congress, the courts, and the public for a type of retroactive approval.

If the unilateral presidency is here to stay—a necessary by-product of the slowness of the separation-of-powers system in operation, a recognition that a war against terrorism and other threats may well be with us for a very long time—does that mean we must remain vulnerable to one-man rule, that we must institutionalize an imperial presidency? Does permanent crisis create a permanent imperial presidency?

Conclusion

Our faith in presidents as saviors has not always been well placed. If there have been Abraham Lincolns and Franklin D. Roosevelts, there have also been James Buchanans and George W. Bushes. We need a president grounded in the fundamental truths of the framers, yet one who can also meet the challenges of the modern era. There is no panacea. Governing is a process in which humans are called upon to make complex judgments in a confusing world. We will, on occasion, make mistakes. Yet we must try. We must find ways to better serve our interests.

We can do better than merely resigning ourselves to the vicissitudes of a presidential nation. The genius of the framers holds as valid in our age as in theirs. So let us return to a renewed, reformed, and strengthened variant of the separation of powers. It remains our best hope for constitutional and democratic government. As messy, confusing, frustrating, and aggravating as the separation of powers *can be*, it may still offer us the best available model for governing. If made to work properly, the separation of powers, and the theory of government that animates it, offers an opportunity for the government to be both powerful and democratically accountable.

APPENDIX 1:
PRIMARY SOURCES

"Of Monarchy and Hereditary Succession," from *Common Sense* by Thomas Paine

MANKIND being originally equals in the order of creation, the equality could only be destroyed by some subsequent circumstance: the distinctions of rich and poor may in a great measure be accounted for, and that without having recourse to the harsh ill-sounding names of oppression and avarice. Oppression is often the CONSEQUENCE, but seldom or never the MEANS of riches; and tho' avarice will preserve a man from being necessitously poor, it generally makes him too timorous to be wealthy.

But there is another and great distinction for which no truly natural or religious reason can be assigned, and that is the distinction of men into KINGS and SUBJECTS. Male and female are the distinctions of nature, good and bad the distinctions of Heaven; but how a race of men came into the world so exalted above the rest, and distinguished like some new species, is worth inquiring into, and whether they are the means of happiness or of misery to mankind.

In the early ages of the world, according to the scripture chronology there were no kings; the consequence of which was, there were no wars; it is the pride of kings which throws mankind into confusion. Holland, without a king hath enjoyed more peace for this last century than any of the monarchical governments in Europe. Antiquity favours the same remark; for the quiet and rural lives of the first Patriarchs have a snappy something in them, which vanishes when we come to the history of Jewish royalty.

Government by kings was first introduced into the world by the Heathens, from whom the children of Israel copied the custom. It was the most prosperous invention the Devil ever set on foot for the promotion of idolatry. The Heathens paid divine honours to their deceased kings, and the Christian World hath improved on the plan by doing the same to their living ones. How impious is the title of sacred Majesty applied to a worm, who in the midst of his splendor is crumbling into dust!

As the exalting one man so greatly above the rest cannot be justified on the equal rights of nature, so neither can it be defended on the authority of scripture; for the will of the Almighty as declared by Gideon, and the prophet Samuel, expressly disapproves of government by Kings.

All anti-monarchical parts of scripture have been very smoothly glossed over in monarchical governments, but they undoubtedly merit the attention of countries which have their governments yet to form. "Render unto Cesar the things which are Cesar's" is the scripture doctrine of courts, yet it is no support of monarchical government, for the Jews at that time were without a king, and in a state of vassalage to the Romans.

Near three thousand years passed away, from the Mosaic account of the creation, till the Jews under a national delusion requested a king. Till then their form of government (except in extraordinary cases where the Almighty interposed) was a kind of Republic, administered by a judge and the elders of the tribes. Kings they had none, and it was held sinful to acknowledge any being under that title but the Lord of Hosts. And when a man seriously reflects on the idolatrous homage which is paid to the persons of kings, he need not wonder that the Almighty, ever jealous of his honour, should disapprove a form of government which so impiously invades the prerogative of Heaven.

Monarchy is ranked in scripture as one of the sins of the Jews, for which a curse in reserve is denounced against them. The history of that transaction is worth attending to.

The children of Israel being oppressed by the Midianites, Gideon marched against them with a small army, and victory thro' the divine interposition decided in his favour. The Jews, elate with success, and attributing it to the generalship of Gideon, proposed making him a king, saying, "Rule thou over us, thou and thy son, and thy son's son." Here was temptation in its fullest extent; not a kingdom only, but an hereditary one; but Gideon in the piety of his soul replied, "I will not rule over you, neither shall my son rule over you. THE LORD SHALL RULE OVER YOU." Words need not be more explicit: Gideon doth not decline the honour, but denieth their right to give it; neither doth he compliment them with invented declarations of his thanks, but in the positive style of a prophet charges them with disaffection to their proper Sovereign, the King of Heaven.

About one hundred and thirty years after this, they fell again into the same error. The hankering which the Jews had for the idolatrous customs of the Heathens, is something exceedingly unaccountable; but so it was, that laying hold of the misconduct of Samuel's two sons, who were intrusted with some secular concerns, they came in an abrupt and clamorous manner to Samuel, saying, "Behold thou art old, and thy sons walk not in thy ways, now make us a king to judge us like all the other nations." And here we cannot observe but that their motives were bad, viz. that they might be LIKE unto other nations, i.e. the Heathens, whereas their true glory lay in being as much UNLIKE them as possible. But the thing displeased Samuel when they said, give us a King to judge us; and Samuel prayed unto the Lord, and the Lord said unto Samuel, hearken unto the voice of the people in all that they say unto thee, for they have not rejected thee, but they have rejected me, THAT I SHOULD NOT REIGN OVER THEM. According to all the works which they have done since the day that I brought them up out of Egypt even unto this day, wherewith they have forsaken me, and served other Gods: so do they also unto thee. Now therefore hearken unto their voice, howbeit, protest solemnly unto them and show them the manner of the King that shall reign over them," i.e., not of any particular King, but the general manner of the Kings of the earth whom Israel was so eagerly copying after. And notwithstanding the great distance of time and difference of manners, the character is still in fashion. And Samuel told all the words of the Lord unto the people, that asked of him a King. And he said, "This shall be the manner of the King that shall reign over you. He will take your sons and appoint them for himself for his chariots and to be his horsemen, and some shall run before his chariots" (this description agrees with the present mode of impressing men) "and he will appoint him captains over thousands and captains over fifties, will set them to clear his ground and to reap his harvest, and to make his instruments of war, and instruments of his chariots, And he will take your daughters to be confectionaries, and to be cooks, and to be bakers" (this describes the expense and luxury as well as the oppression of Kings) "and he will take your fields and your vineyards, and your olive yards, even the best of them, and give them to his servants. And he will take the tenth of your seed, and of your vineyards, and give them to his officers and to his servants" (by which we see that bribery, corruption, and favouritism, are the standing vices of Kings) "and he will take the tenth of your men servants, and your maid servants, and your goodliest young men, and your asses, and put them to his work: and he will take the tenth of your sheep, and ye shall be his servants, and ye shall cry out in that day because of your king which ye shell have chosen, AND

THE LORD WILL NOT HEAR YOU IN THAT DAY." This accounts for the continuation of Monarchy; neither do the characters of the few good kings which have lived since, either sanctify the title, or blot out the sinfulness of the origin; the high encomium of David takes no notice of him OFFICIALLY AS A KING, but only as a MAN after God's own heart. Nevertheless the people refused to obey the voice of Samuel, and they said, "Nay, but we will have a king over us, that we may be like all the nations, and that our king may judge us, and go out before us and fight our battles." Samuel continued to reason with them but to no purpose; he set before them their ingratitude, but all would not avail; and seeing them fully bent on their folly, he cried out, "I will call unto the Lord, and he shall send thunder and rain" (which was then a punishment, being in the time of wheat harvest) "that ye may perceive and see that your wickedness is great which ye have done in the sight of the Lord, IN ASKING YOU A KING. So Samuel called unto the Lord, and the Lord sent thunder and rain that day, and all the people greatly feared the Lord and Samuel. And all the people said unto Samuel, Pray for thy servants unto the Lord thy God that we die not, for WE HAVE ADDED UNTO OUR SINS THIS EVIL, TO ASK A KING." These portions of scripture are direct and positive. They admit of no equivocal construction. That the Almighty hath here entered his protest against monarchical government is true, or the scripture is false. And a man hath good reason to believe that there is as much of kingcraft as priestcraft in withholding the scripture from the public in popish countries. For monarchy in every instance is the popery of government.

To the evil of monarchy we have added that of hereditary succession; and as the first is a degradation and lessening of ourselves, so the second, claimed as a matter of right, is an insult and imposition on posterity. For all men being originally equals, no one by birth could have a right to set up his own family in perpetual preference to all others for ever, and tho' himself might deserve some decent degree of honours of his contemporaries, yet his descendants might be far too unworthy to inherit them. One of the strongest natural proofs of the folly of hereditary right in Kings, is that nature disapproves it, otherwise she would not so frequently turn it into ridicule, by giving mankind an ASS FOR A LION.

Secondly, as no man at first could possess any other public honors than were bestowed upon him, so the givers of those honors could have no power to give away the right of posterity, and though they might say "We choose you for our head," they could not without manifest injustice to their children say "that your children and your children's children shall reign over ours forever." Because such an unwise, unjust, unnatural compact might (perhaps) in the next succession put them under the government of a rogue or a fool. Most wise men in their private sentiments have ever treated hereditary right with contempt; yet it is one of those evils which when once established is not easily removed: many submit from fear, others from superstition, and the more powerful part shares with the king the plunder of the rest.

This is supposing the present race of kings in the world to have had an honorable origin: whereas it is more than probable, that, could we take off the dark covering of antiquity and trace them to their first rise, we should find the first of them nothing better than the principal ruffian of some restless gang, whose savage manners of pre-eminence in subtilty obtained him the title of chief among plunderers; and who by increasing in power and extending his depredations, overawed the quiet and defenseless to purchase their safety by frequent contributions. Yet his electors could have no idea of giving hereditary right to his descendants, because such a perpetual exclusion of themselves was incompatible with the free and restrained principles they professed to live by. Wherefore, hereditary succession in the early ages of monarchy could not take place as a matter of claim, but as something casual or complemental; but as few or no records were extant in those days, the traditionary history stuff'd with fables, it was very easy, after the lapse of a few generations, to trump up some superstitious tale conveniently timed, Mahomet-like, to cram hereditary right down the throats of the vulgar. Perhaps the disorders which threatened, or seemed to threaten, on the decease of a leader and the choice of a new one (for elections among ruffians could not be very orderly) induced many at first to favour hereditary pretensions; by which means it happened, as it hath happened since, that what at first was submitted to as a convenience was afterwards claimed as a right.

England since the conquest hath known some few good monarchs, but groaned beneath a much larger number of bad ones: yet no man in his senses can say that their claim under William the Conqueror is a very honourable one. A French bastard landing with an armed Banditti and establishing himself king of England against the consent of the natives, is in plain terms a very paltry rascally original. It certainly hath no divinity in it. However it is needless to spend much time in exposing the folly of hereditary right; if there are any so weak as to believe it, let them promiscuously worship the Ass and the Lion, and welcome. I shall neither copy their humility, nor disturb their devotion.

Yet I should be glad to ask how they suppose kings came at first? The question admits but of three answers, viz. either by lot, by election, or by usurpation. If the first king was taken by lot, it establishes a precedent for the next, which excludes hereditary succession. Saul was by lot, yet the succession was not hereditary, neither does it appear from that transaction that there was any intention it ever should. If the first king of any country was by election, that likewise establishes a precedent for the next; for to say, that the right of all future generations is taken away, by the act of the first electors, in their choice not only of a king but of a family of kings for ever, hath no parallel in or out of scripture but the doctrine of original sin, which supposes the free will of all men lost in Adam; and from such comparison, and it will admit of no other, hereditary succession can derive no glory. For as in Adam all sinned, and as in the first electors all men obeyed; as in the one all mankind were subjected to Satan, and in the other to sovereignty; as our innocence was lost in the first, and our authority in the last; and as both disable us from re-assuming some former state and privilege, it unanswerably follows that original sin and hereditary succession are parallels. Dishonourable rank! inglorious connection! yet the most subtle sophist cannot produce a juster simile.

As to usurpation, no man will be so hardy as to defend it; and that William the Conqueror was an usurper is a fact not to be contradicted. The plain truth is, that the antiquity of English monarchy will not bear looking into.

But it is not so much the absurdity as the evil of hereditary succession which concerns mankind. Did it ensure a race of good and wise men it would have the seal of divine authority, but as it opens a door to the FOOLISH, the WICKED, and the IMPROPER, it hath in it the nature of oppression. Men who look upon themselves born to reign, and others to obey, soon grow insolent. Selected from the rest of mankind, their minds are early poisoned by importance; and the world they act in differs so materially from the world at large, that they have but little opportunity of knowing its true interests, and when they succeed in the government are frequently the most ignorant and unfit of any throughout the dominions.

Another evil which attends hereditary succession is, that the throne is subject to be possessed by a minor at any age; all which time the regency acting under the cover of a king have every opportunity and inducement to betray their trust. The same national misfortune happens when a king worn out with age and infirmity enters the last stage of human weakness. In both these cases the public becomes a prey to every miscreant who can tamper successfully with the follies either of age or infancy.

The most plausible plea which hath ever been offered in favor of hereditary succession is, that it preserves a nation from civil wars; and were this true, it would be weighty; whereas it is the most bare-faced falsity ever imposed upon mankind. The whole history of England disowns the fact. Thirty kings and two minors have reigned in that distracted kingdom since the conquest, in which time there has been (including the revolution) no less than eight civil wars and nineteen Rebellions. Wherefore instead of making for peace, it makes against it, and destroys the very foundation it seems to stand upon.

The contest for monarchy and succession, between the houses of York and Lancaster, laid England in a scene of blood for many years. Twelve pitched battles besides skirmishes and sieges were fought between Henry and Edward. Twice was Henry prisoner to Edward, who in his turn was prisoner to Henry. And so uncertain is the fate of war and the temper of a nation, when nothing but personal matters are the ground of a quarrel, that Henry was taken in triumph from a prison to a palace, and Edward obliged to fly from a palace to a foreign land; yet, as sudden transitions of temper are seldom lasting, Henry in his turn was driven from the throne, and Edward re-called to succeed him. The parliament always following the strongest side.

This contest began in the reign of Henry the Sixth, and was not entirely extinguished till Henry the Seventh, in whom the families were united. Including a period of 67 years, viz. from 1422 to 1489.

In short, monarchy and succession have laid (not this or that kingdom only) but the world in blood and ashes. 'Tis a form of government which the word of God bears testimony against, and blood will attend it.

If we enquire into the business of a King, we shall find that in some countries they may have none; and after sauntering away their lives without pleasure to themselves or advantage to the nation, withdraw from the scene, and leave their successors to tread the same idle round. In absolute monarchies the whole weight of business civil and military lies on the King; the children of Israel in their request for a king urged this plea, "that he may judge us, and go out before us and fight our battles." But in countries where he is neither a Judge nor a General, as in England, a man would be puzzled to know what IS his business.

The nearer any government approaches to a Republic, the less business there is for a King. It is somewhat difficult to find a proper name for the government of England. Sir William Meredith calls it a Republic; but in its present state it is unworthy of the name, because the corrupt influence of the Crown, by having all the places in its disposal, hath so effectually swallowed up the power, and eaten out the virtue of the House of Commons (the Republican part in the constitution) that the government of England is nearly as monarchical as that of France or Spain. Men fall out with names without understanding them. For 'tis the Republican and not the Monarchical part of the Constitution of England which Englishmen glory in, viz. the liberty of choosing an House of Commons from out of their own body—and it is easy to see that when Republican virtues fail, slavery ensues. Why is the constitution of England sickly, but because monarchy hath poisoned the Republic; the Crown hath engrossed the Commons.

In England a King hath little more to do than to make war and give away places; which, in plain terms, is to impoverish the nation and set it together by the ears. A pretty business indeed for a man to be allowed eight hundred thousand sterling a year for, and worshipped into the bargain! Of more worth is one honest man to society, and in the sight of God, than all the crowned ruffians that ever lived.

The Declaration of Independence

In Congress, July 4, 1776

The unanimous Declaration of the thirteen united States of America,

When in the Course of human events, it becomes necessary for one people to dissolve the political bands which have connected them with another, and to assume among the powers of the earth, the separate and equal station to which the Laws of Nature and of Nature's God entitle them, a decent respect to the opinions of mankind requires that they should declare the causes which impel them to the separation.

We hold these truths to be self-evident, that all men are created equal, that they are endowed by their Creator with certain unalienable Rights, that among these are Life, Liberty and the pursuit of Happiness.—That to secure these rights, Governments are instituted among Men, deriving their just powers from the consent of the Governed,—that whenever any Form of Government becomes destructive of these ends, it is the Right of the People to alter or to abolish it, and to institute new Government, laying its foundation on such principles and organizing its powers in such form, as to them shall seem most likely to effect their Safety and Happiness. Prudence, indeed, will dictate that Governments long established should not be changed for light and transient causes; and accordingly all experience hath shewn, that mankind are more disposed to suffer, while evils are sufferable, than to right themselves by abolishing the forms to which they are accustomed. But when a long train of Abuses and Usurpations, pursuing invariably the same Object, evinces a design to reduce them under absolute Despotism, it is their right, it is their duty, to throw off such Government, and to provide new Guards for their future security.—Such has been the patient sufferance of these Colonies; and such is now the necessity which constrains them to alter their former Systems of Government. The history of the present King of Great Britain is a history of repeated injuries and usurpations, all having in direct object the establishment of an absolute Tyranny over these States. To prove this, let Facts be submitted to a candid world.

He has refused his Assent to Laws, the most wholesome and necessary for the public good.

He has forbidden his Governors to pass Laws of immediate and pressing importance, unless suspended in their operation till his Assent should be obtained; and when so suspended, he has utterly neglected to attend to them.

He has refused to pass other Laws for the accommodation of large districts of people, unless those people would relinquish the right of Representation in the Legislature, a right inestimable to them and formidable to tyrants only.

He has called together legislative bodies at places unusual, uncomfortable, and distant from the depository of their public Records, for the sole purpose of fatiguing them into compliance with his measures.

He has dissolved Representative Houses repeatedly, for opposing with manly firmness his invasions on the rights of the people.

He has refused for a long time, after such dissolutions, to cause others to be elected; whereby the Legislative powers, incapable of Annihilation, have returned to the People at large for their exercise; the State remaining in the mean time exposed to all the dangers of invasion from without, and convulsions within.

He has endeavoured to prevent the population of these States; for that purpose obstructing the Laws for Naturalization of Foreigners; refusing to pass others to encourage their migrations hither, and raising the conditions of new Appropriations of Lands.

He has obstructed the Administration of Justice, by refusing his Assent to Laws for establishing Judiciary powers.

He has made Judges dependent on his Will alone, for the tenure of their offices, and the amount and payment of their salaries.

He has erected a multitude of New Offices, and sent hither swarms of Officers to harrass our people, and eat out their substance.

He has kept among us, in times of peace, Standing Armies without the Consent of our legislatures.

He has affected to render the Military independent of and superior to the Civil power.

He has combined with others to subject us to a jurisdiction foreign to our constitution, and unacknowledged by our laws; giving his Assent to their Acts of pretended Legislation:

For Quartering large bodies of armed troops among us:

For protecting them, by a mock Trial, from punishment for any Murders which they should commit on the Inhabitants of these States:

For cutting off our Trade with all parts of the world:

For imposing Taxes on us without our Consent:

For depriving us in many cases, of the benefits of Trial by Jury:

For transporting us beyond Seas to be tried for pretended offences:

For abolishing the free System of English Laws in a neighbouring Province, establishing therein an Arbitrary government, and enlarging its Boundaries so as to render it at once an example and fit instrument for introducing the same absolute rule into these Colonies:

For taking away our Charters, abolishing our most valuable Laws, and altering fundamentally the Forms of our Governments:

For suspending our own Legislatures, and declaring themselves invested with power to legislate for us in all cases whatsoever.

He has abdicated Government here, by declaring us out of his Protection and waging War against us.

He has plundered our seas, ravaged our Coasts, burnt our towns, and destroyed the lives of our people.

He is at this time transporting large Armies of foreign Mercenaries to compleat the works of death, desolation and tyranny, already begun with circumstances of Cruelty & perfidy scarcely paralleled in the most barbarous ages, and totally unworthy the Head of a civilized nation.

He has constrained our fellow Citizens taken Captive on the high Seas to bear Arms against their Country, to become the executioners of their friends and Brethren, or to fall themselves by their Hands.

He has excited domestic insurrections amongst us, and has endeavoured to bring on the inhabitants of our frontiers, the merciless Indian Savages, whose known rule of warfare, is an undistinguished destruction of all ages, sexes and conditions.

In every stage of these Oppressions We have Petitioned for Redress in the most humble terms: Our repeated Petitions have been answered only by repeated injury. A Prince whose character is thus marked by every act which may define a Tyrant, is unfit to be the ruler of a free people.

Nor have We been wanting in Attentions to our British Brethren. We have warned them from Time to Time of Attempts by their Legislature to extend an unwarrantable Jurisdiction over us. We have reminded them of the Circumstances of our emigration and settlement here. We have appealed to their native Justice and Magnanimity, and we have conjured them by the ties of our common kindred to disavow these Usurpations, which, would inevitably interrupt our connections and correspondence. They too have been deaf to the voice of justice and of consanguinity. We must, therefore, acquiesce in the necessity, which denounces our Separation, and hold them, as we hold the rest of mankind, Enemies in War, in Peace Friends.

We, therefore, the Representatives of the united States of America, in General Congress, Assembled, appealing to the Supreme

Judge of the world for the rectitude of our intentions, do, in the Name, and by Authority of the good People of these Colonies, solemnly publish and declare, That these United Colonies are, and of Right ought to be Free and Independent States; that they are Absolved from all Allegiance to the British Crown, and that all political connection between them and the State of Great Britain, is and ought to be totally dissolved; and that as Free and Independent States, they have full Power to levy War, conclude Peace, contract Alliances, establish Commerce, and to do all other Acts and Things which Independent States may of right do. And for the support of this Declaration, with a firm reliance on the protection of divine Providence, we mutually pledge to each other our Lives, our Fortunes and our sacred Honor.

The United States Constitution, Article II

Section 1

The executive Power shall be vested in a President of the United States of America. He shall hold his Office during the Term of four Years, and, together with the Vice President, chosen for the same Term, be elected, as follows:

Each State shall appoint, in such Manner as the Legislature thereof may direct, a Number of Electors, equal to the whole Number of Senators and Representatives to which the State may be entitled in the Congress: but no Senator or Representative, or Person holding an Office of Trust or Profit under the United States, shall be appointed an Elector.

The Electors shall meet in their respective States, and vote by Ballot for two Persons, of whom one at least shall not be an Inhabitant of the same State with themselves. And they shall make a List of all the Persons voted for, and of the Number of Votes for each; which List they shall sign and certify, and transmit sealed to the Seat of the Government of the United States, directed to the President of the Senate. The President of the Senate shall, in the Presence of the Senate and House of Representatives, open all the Certificates, and the Votes shall then be counted. The Person having the greatest Number of Votes shall be the President, if such Number be a Majority of the whole Number of Electors appointed; and if there be more than one who have such Majority, and have an equal Number of Votes, then the House of Representatives shall immediately chuse by Ballot one of them for President; and if no Person have a Majority, then from the five highest on the List the said House shall in like Manner chuse the President. But in chusing the President, the Votes shall be taken by States, the Representation from each State having one Vote; A quorum for this purpose shall consist of a Member or Members from two thirds of the States, and a Majority of all the States shall be necessary to a Choice. In every Case, after the Choice of the President, the Person having the greatest Number of Votes of the Electors shall be the Vice President. But if there should remain two or more who have equal Votes, the Senate shall chuse from them by Ballot the Vice President.

The Congress may determine the Time of chusing the Electors, and the Day on which they shall give their Votes; which Day shall be the same throughout the United States.

No Person except a natural born Citizen, or a Citizen of the United States, at the time of the Adoption of this Constitution, shall be eligible to the Office of President; neither shall any Person be eligible to that Office who shall not have attained to the Age of thirty five Years, and been fourteen Years a Resident within the United States.

In Case of the Removal of the President from Office, or of his Death, Resignation, or Inability to discharge the Powers and Duties of the said Office, the Same shall devolve on the Vice President, and the Congress may by Law provide for the Case of Removal,

Death, Resignation or Inability, both of the President and Vice President, declaring what Officer shall then act as President, and such Officer shall act accordingly, until the Disability be removed, or a President shall be elected.

The President shall, at stated Times, receive for his Services, a Compensation, which shall neither be increased nor diminished during the Period for which he shall have been elected, and he shall not receive within that Period any other Emolument from the United States, or any of them.

Before he enter on the Execution of his Office, he shall take the following Oath or Affirmation:—"I do solemnly swear (or affirm) that I will faithfully execute the Office of President of the United States, and will to the best of my Ability, preserve, protect and defend the Constitution of the United States."

Section 2

The President shall be Commander in Chief of the Army and Navy of the United States, and of the Militia of the several States, when called into the actual Service of the United States; he may require the Opinion, in writing, of the principal Officer in each of the executive Departments, upon any Subject relating to the Duties of their respective Offices, and he shall have Power to grant Reprieves and Pardons for Offences against the United States, except in Cases of Impeachment.

He shall have Power, by and with the Advice and Consent of the Senate, to make Treaties, provided two thirds of the Senators present concur; and he shall nominate, and by and with the Advice and Consent of the Senate, shall appoint Ambassadors, other public Ministers and Consuls, Judges of the supreme Court, and all other Officers of the United States, whose Appointments are not herein otherwise provided for, and which shall be established by Law: but the Congress may by Law vest the Appointment of such inferior Officers, as they think proper, in the President alone, in the Courts of Law, or in the Heads of Departments.

The President shall have Power to fill up all Vacancies that may happen during the Recess of the Senate, by granting Commissions which shall expire at the End of their next Session.

Section 3

He shall from time to time give to the Congress Information of the State of the Union, and recommend to their Consideration such Measures as he shall judge necessary and expedient; he may, on extraordinary Occasions, convene both Houses, or either of them, and in Case of Disagreement between them, with Respect to the Time of Adjournment, he may adjourn them to such Time as he shall think proper; he shall receive Ambassadors and other public Ministers; he shall take Care that the Laws be faithfully executed, and shall Commission all the Officers of the United States.

Section 4

The President, Vice President and all civil Officers of the United States, shall be removed from Office on Impeachment for, and Conviction of, Treason, Bribery, or other high Crimes and Misdemeanors.

Gettysburg Address

Fourscore and seven years ago our fathers brought forth on this continent a new nation, conceived in liberty and dedicated to the proposition that all men are created equal. Now we are engaged in a great civil war, testing whether that nation or any nation so conceived and so dedicated can long endure. We are met on a great battlefield of that war. We have come to dedicate a portion of that field as a final resting-place for those who here gave their lives that that nation might live. It is altogether fitting and proper that we should do this. But in a larger sense, we cannot dedicate, we cannot consecrate, we cannot hallow this ground. The brave men, living and dead who struggled here have consecrated it far above our poor power to add or detract. The world will little note nor long remember what we say here, but it can never forget what they did here. It is for us the living rather to be dedicated here to the unfinished work which they who fought here have thus far so nobly advanced. It is rather for us to be here dedicated to the great task remaining before us—that from these honored dead we take increased devotion to that cause for which they gave the last full measure of devotion—that we here highly resolve that these dead shall not have died in vain, that this nation under God shall have a new birth of freedom, and that government of the people, by the people, for the people shall not perish from the earth.

Abraham Lincoln's Second Inaugural Address

Fellow Countrymen:

At this second appearing to take the oath of the presidential office, there is less occasion for an extended address than there was at the first. Then a statement, somewhat in detail, of a course to be pursued, seemed fitting and proper. Now, at the expiration of four years, during which public declarations have been constantly called forth on every point and phase of the great contest which still absorbs the attention, and engrosses the energies of the nation, little that is new could be presented. The progress of our arms, upon which all else chiefly depends, is as well known to the public as to myself; and it is, I trust, reasonably satisfactory and encouraging to all. With high hope for the future, no prediction in regard to it is ventured.

On the occasion corresponding to this four years ago, all thoughts were anxiously directed to an impending civil-war. All dreaded it— all sought to avert it. While the inaugural address was being delivered from this place, devoted altogether to *saving* the Union without war, insurgent agents were in the city seeking to *destroy* it without war—seeking to dissolve the Union, and divide effects, by negotiation. Both parties deprecated war; but one of them would *make* war rather than let the nation survive; and the other would *accept* war rather than let it perish. And the war came.

One eighth of the whole population were colored slaves, not distributed generally over the Union, but localized in the Southern part of it. These slaves constituted a peculiar and powerful interest. All knew that this interest was, somehow, the cause of the war. To strengthen, perpetuate, and extend this interest was the object for which the insurgents would rend the Union, even by war; while the government claimed no right to do more than to restrict the territorial enlargement of it. Neither party expected for the war, the magnitude, or the duration, which it has already attained. Neither anticipated that the *cause* of the conflict might cease with, or even before, the conflict itself should cease. Each looked for an easier triumph, and a result less fundamental and astounding. Both read the same Bible, and pray to the same God; and each invokes His aid against the other. It may seem strange that any men should dare to ask a just God's assistance in wringing their bread from the sweat of other men's faces; but let us judge not that we be not judged. The prayers of both could not be answered; that of neither has been answered fully. The Almighty has His own purposes. "Woe unto the world because of offences! for it must needs be that offences come; but woe to that man by whom the offence cometh!" If we shall suppose that American Slavery is one of those offences which, in the providence of God, must needs come, but which, having continued through His appointed time, He now wills to remove, and that He gives to both North and South, this terrible war, as the woe due to those by whom the offence came, shall we discern therein any departure from those divine attributes which the believers in a Living God always ascribe to Him? Fondly do we hope—fervently do we pray—that this mighty scourge of war may speedily pass away. Yet, if God wills that it continue, until all the wealth piled by the bondman's two hundred and fifty years of unrequited toil shall be sunk, and until every drop of blood drawn with the lash, shall be paid by another drawn with the sword, as was said three thousand years ago, so still it must be said "the judgments of the Lord, are true and righteous altogether."

With malice toward none; with charity for all; with firmness in the right, as God gives us to see the right, let us strive on to finish the work we are in; to bind up the nation's wounds; to care for him who shall have borne the battle, and for his widow, and his orphan—to do all which may achieve and cherish a just, and a lasting peace, among ourselves, and with all nations.

APPENDIX 2:
UNDERSTANDING THE FORCES THAT
IMPACT PRESIDENTIAL LEADERSHIP

Presidential leadership (as opposed to the exercise of raw power) is grounded in the interconnection between *structure, context, resources, and skill.*[1] *Context* (sometimes called *level of political opportunity*) refers to political conditions under which the president operates. Is there a *war* or *crisis*, or does the president govern in *neutral* or *routine* times? In a crisis, the president's power expands dramatically; in normal times, it contracts. Is the president dealing with foreign or domestic affairs? Generally, the president will have greater authority to act in foreign affairs than in the domestic arena.

Putting structure, context, resources, and skill together is a tricky task. However, in an effort to get to the core of presidential leadership, I offer a pretheoretical dyadic model of presidential leadership designed to both highlight the key variables that help us understand leadership and *predict* levels of presidential power (see Table A.1).

The model suggests an interrelationship between key variables, organized as dyads for theoretical and predictive utility. This model is offered as a "pretheory" to build toward a theory of the presidency. In this model, the dependent variable is "power." We want to understand

TABLE A.1
A DYADIC MODEL OF PRESIDENTIAL POWER

CONDITION	CRISIS																ROUTINE															
POLICY AREA	FOREIGN POLICY								DOMESTIC POLICY								FOREIGN POLICY								DOMESTIC POLICY							
CONGRESSIONAL MAJORITY	UNIFIED GOVERNMENT		DIVIDED GOVERNMENT		UNIFIED GOVERNMENT		DIVIDED GOVERNMENT		UNIFIED GOVERNMENT		DIVIDED GOVERNMENT		UNIFIED GOVERNMENT		DIVIDED GOVERNMENT		UNIFIED GOVERNMENT		DIVIDED GOVERNMENT		UNIFIED GOVERNMENT		DIVIDED GOVERNMENT		UNIFIED GOVERNMENT		DIVIDED GOVERNMENT		UNIFIED GOVERNMENT		DIVIDED GOVERNMENT	
PRESIDENTIAL INITIATIVE/ RESPONSE	ACTIVIST				RESTRAINED				ACTIVIST				RESTRAINED				ACTIVIST				RESTRAINED				ACTIVIST				RESTRAINED			
PRESIDENTIAL SKILL	HIGH	LOW	HIGH	LOW	HIGH	LOW	HIGH	LOW	HIGH	LOW	HIGH	LOW	HIGH	LOW	HIGH	LOW	HIGH	LOW	HIGH	LOW	HIGH	LOW	HIGH	LOW	HIGH	LOW	HIGH	LOW	HIGH	LOW	HIGH	LOW
	1	2	3	4	5	6	7	8	9	10	11	12	13	14	15	16	17	18	19	20	21	22	23	24	25	26	27	28	29	30	31	32

HIGHEST ——————————————— POWER ——————————————— LOWEST

and explain when presidents are more and less powerful. We then present six independent variables that account for—in order of significance—variations in the dependent variable. At the bottom of the model, I suggest thirty-two levels of power resulting from the model. These levels suggest hypotheses that can be tested.

The first and most important relationship is the *crisis versus routine* dyad, which asserts that presidents exert more power and authority in crisis versus noncrisis situations. Political scientists have long noted that during a crisis, the restraining web of the checks and balances comes unglued, and we defer power to the executive. Although crises may be few and far between, it is clear that during an emergency, the power of the presidency swells and the influence of Congress recedes.

The second dyad is the *foreign versus domestic* policy relationship, with the assumption being that presidents wield greater authority in foreign than domestic affairs. Again, political scientists, starting with the seminal work by Aaron Wildavsky, have noted that presidents usually have greater power in foreign affairs than over domestic or economic policy. Although this power may be constitutionally questionable, it has become the political reality.

Third is the *partisan membership of Congress*, wherein a president should be more powerful when his party controls Congress. While divided government does not necessarily mean deadlocked government, it is clear that a president with a commanding congressional majority has smoother political sailing than a president who faces a Congress controlled by the opposition party.

The fourth *level of presidential response* is important, with a more activist president exerting more power than a president of restraint. Presidents who appear weak and hesitant, who seem paralyzed by high-stress situations, tend to lose respect rather quickly. Americans like a firm, even tough, response to troubles and expect presidents to "take charge" and be the nation's problem solver.

The fifth set of variables is *skill* level, with *high* skill resulting in greater power than low, or more limited, skill. Although it may seem obvious to assert that skill matters, it must be noted that skill is not enough. Highly skilled presidents facing low-opportunity situations may be more circumscribed than lower-skilled presidents who face high-opportunity settings.

Each level of the model of presidential leadership connects to the others, leading one down the scale to the scores at the bottom of the table. Those scores predict the level of power a president will have in each of the relationships. For example, one expects the president to be most powerful in box 1: a crisis in foreign policy where the president is highly skilled and has the position backing of the dominant party in Congress and when the president is highly popular and exerts an activist approach to the problem at hand. Conversely, the president is *least* able to exert leadership in box 64: in routine domestic affairs, where the president's skills are limited, facing a Congress controlled by the opposition party, when the president has low popularity ratings and takes a more restrained approach to confronting the problem.

NOTES

Chapter 1

1. See John Yoo, *War by Other Means.*

2. See, for example, Melanie Marlowe, "The Unitary Executive."

3. See Eric A. Posner and Adrian Vermeule, *The Executive Unbound: After The Madisonian Republic.*

4. See Harold Hongju Koh, *The National Security Constitution: Sharing Power After the Iran-Contra Affair.*

5. See Thomas E. Cronin and Michael A. Genovese, *The Paradoxes of the American Presidency.*

6. Scott M. Matheson Jr., *Presidential Constitutionalism in Perilous Times.*

Chapter 2

1. See Barbara W. Tuchman, "The British Lose America," 127–231.

2. Scott Liell, *46 Pages: Thomas Paine,* Common Sense, *and the Turning Point to Independence,* 15, 17.

3. Quoted in Matthew Spalding, *The Founder's Almanac,* 215.

4. Bernard Bailyn, *The Ideological Origins of the American Revolution.*

5. Charles C. Thach, *The Creation of the Presidency, 1775–1789: A Study in Constitutional History.*

6. Quoted in Cyril C. Means Jr., "Is Presidency Barred to Americans Born Abroad?"

7. Thomas E. Cronin, ed., *Inventing the American Presidency.*

8. Ralph Ketcham, *Presidents Above Party,* 9.

9. Alan Wolfe, "Presidential Power and the Crisis of Modernization," 21.

10. Charles Beard and Mary Beard, *The Rise of American Civilization,* 317.

11. For a full examination of the constitutional presidency, see David Gray Adler, "The Constitutional Presidency."

12. *Youngstown Sheet & Tube Co. v. Sawyer*, 343 US 5789, 635 (1952).

13. Edward S. Corwin, *The President: Office and Powers, 1787–1984*. See also Joseph M. Bessette and Jeffrey Tulis, *The Presidency in the Constitutional Order*; and Louis Fisher, *The Constitution Between Friends*.

14. Bert A. Rockman, *The Leadership Question: The Presidency and the American System*, 39, 40, 41.

15. Ibid., 43.

16. Yoo, *War by Other Means*, chap. 5.

17. See Michael A. Genovese, *Presidential Prerogative: Imperial Power in an Age of Terrorism*.

18. Lester J. Cappon, *The Adams-Jefferson Letters: The Complete Correspondence Between Thomas Jefferson and Abigail and John Adams*, 212.

Chapter 3

1. This chapter and the next are, in part, a distillation of parts of my earlier book *The Power of the American Presidency, 1789–2000*.

2. See Cronin and Genovese, *Paradoxes of the American Presidency*.

3. See ibid.

4. See Arthur M. Schlesinger Jr., *War and the American Presidency*, 47.

5. Abraham Lincoln, "Special Session Message, July 4, 1861," in *A Compilation of the Messages and Papers of the Presidents*.

6. Jay S. Bybee, Assistant Attorney General, US Department of Justice, "Memorandum for Alberto R. Gonzales"; "Working Group Report on Detainee Interrogations in the Global War on Terrorism: Assessment of Legal, Historical, Policy, and Operational Considerations." The "Working Group Report" was to be declassified in 2013 but was declassified on June 21, 2004, after an earlier draft of the report, dated March 6, 2003, had been leaked to the *Wall Street Journal*. Jess Bravin, "Pentagon Report Sought to Justify Use of Torture," *Wall Street Journal*, June 7, 2004, A1.

7. Richard Norton Smith, *Patriarch: George Washington and the New Nation*; James Thomas Flexner, *Washington: The Indispensible Man*; Richard Brookhiser, *Founding Father: Rediscovering George Washington*.

8. Quoted in Norman K. Risjord, *Thomas Jefferson*, 129–130.

9. Merrill D. Peterson, *Thomas Jefferson and the New Nation*.

10. Quoted in Noble E. Cunningham Jr., *In Pursuit of Reason: The Life of Thomas Jefferson*.

11. See Donald L. Robinson, *"To the Best of My Ability": The Presidency and the Constitution*, 45–46.

12. Thomas Jefferson, *Notes on the State of Virginia*, 113, 198–199.

13. See David N. Mayer, "Jefferson and Separation of Powers," 26.

14. See Jeremy David Bailey, "Executive Prerogative and the 'Good Officer' in Thomas Jefferson's Letter to John B. Colvin."

15. Wilson Whitman, arr., *Jefferson's Letters*, 216.

16. Peterson, *Jefferson and the New Nation*, 775. See also Barry J. Balleck, "When the Ends Justify the Means: Thomas Jefferson and the Louisiana Purchase."

17. Quoted in Clinton Rossiter, *Constitutional Dictatorship: Crisis Government in the Modern Democracies*, 12.

18. *Annals of Congress*, 15C15, 1373, March 13, 1817.

19. See Richard Latner, *The Presidency of Andrew Jackson: White House Politics, 1829–1837*; Robert V. Remini, *Andrew Jackson and the Course of American Empire, 1767–1821*; Robert V. Remini, *Andrew Jackson and the Course of American Freedom, 1822–1832*; Robert V. Remini, *Andrew Jackson and the Course of American Democracy, 1833–1845*; Arthur M. Schlesinger Jr., *The Age of Jackson*; and Leonard White, *The Jacksonians: A Study in Administrative History, 1829–1861*.

20. Corwin, *President*, 21.

21. Schlesinger, *The Age of Jackson*, 276.

22. Gary L. Rose, *The American Presidency Under Siege*, 152.

23. William N. Chambers, "Jackson," 83; Corwin, *President*, 21.

24. Robert J. Spitzer, *The Presidential Veto: Touchstone of the American Presidency*, 33–39.

25. Robert V. Remini, "Election of 1832," 1:516.

26. Alexis de Tocqueville, *Democracy in America*, 394.

27. Corwin, *President*, 20.

28. See Paul H. Bergeron, *The Presidency of James K. Polk*; Eugene I. McCormac, *James K. Polk: A Political Biography*; Charles A. McCoy, *Polk and the Presidency*; and Charles G. Sellers, *James K. Polk: Continentalist, 1843–1846*.

29. J. G. Randall and Richard N. Current, *Lincoln: The President*; David Herbert Donald, *Lincoln*; Phillip Shaw Paludan, *The Presidency of Abraham Lincoln*.

30. Ward H. Lamon, *Recollections of Abraham Lincoln*.

31. Abraham Lincoln, *Abraham Lincoln: Speeches and Writings, 1859–1865*, 585–586.

32. Abraham Lincoln, "Special Session Message, July 4, 1861," in *Borzoi Reader in American Politics*, 593.

33. See Genovese, *Presidential Prerogative*.

34. Rossiter, *Constitutional Dictatorship*.

35. Garry Wills, *Lincoln at Gettysburg: The Words That Remade America*, 145.

36. Bruce Miroff, *Icons of Democracy*.

37. James M. McPherson, *Abraham Lincoln and the Second American Revolution*, viii.

38. Quoted in Philip C. Dolce and George H. Skau, eds., *Power and the Presidency*, 44.

39. Clinton Rossiter, *The Supreme Court and the Commander in Chief*, 23. For a defense of Lincoln's actions, see Mark Neely, *The Fate of Liberty*.

40. Rossiter, *Supreme Court*, 23–25.

41. *Ex Parte Milligan*, 4 Wallace 2, 18 L.Ed., 281 (1866).

42. Rossiter, *Supreme Court*, 34–35, 39.

43. *Prize Cases*, 67 US 2 Black 635, 668–670.

44. See Michael A. Genovese, *The Supreme Court, the Constitution, and Presidential Power*.

45. Dolce and Skau, *Power and the Presidency*, 47.

46. See Robert V. Bruce, *Lincoln and the Tools of War*, and John Hay, *Lincoln and the Civil War*.

Chapter 4

1. James Bryce, *The American Commonwealth*.

2. Just four years before Bryce, an influential book calling the end of the presidency received much attention: Henry Clay Lockwood, *The Abolition of the Presidency*.

3. See Michael A. Genovese, ed., "William McKinley," 334.

4. H. W. Brands, *T. R.: The Last Romantic*; Matthew Miller, *Theodore Roosevelt: A Life*; Lewis L. Gould, *The Presidency of Theodore Roosevelt*.

5. Harold Evans, *The American Century*.

6. See Candice Millard, *The River of Doubt: Theodore Roosevelt's Darkest Journey*.

7. Miroff, *Icons of Democracy*, 161, 164.

8. Arthur Bernon Tourtellot, *The Presidents on the Presidency*, 116.

9. Theodore Roosevelt, *The Works of Theodore Roosevelt*, 490.

10. Theodore Roosevelt, *An Autobiography*, 357.

11. Ibid.

12. William Howard Taft, *The President and His Powers*.

13. Woodrow Wilson, *Congressional Government: A Study in American Politics*.

14. Woodrow Wilson, *Constitutional Government in the United States*, 46, 54, 60, 70–71.

15. See Ray Stannard Baker, *Woodrow Wilson*; Arthur Walworth, *Woodrow Wilson*; Kendrick A. Clements, *The Presidency of Woodrow Wilson*; and August Heckscher, *Woodrow Wilson*.

16. *Myers v. United States*, 272 US 52 (1926).

17. *Humphrey's Executor v. United States*, 295 US 602 (1935).

18. Edward S. Corwin, *Total War and the Constitution*, 91.

19. *Hirabayashi v. United States*, 320 US 81 (1943).

20. *Korematsu v. United States*, 323 US 214 (1944).

21. *Ex Parte Endo*, 323 US 283 (1944).

22. Thomas E. Cronin, *The State of the Presidency*.

23. Mary Stuckey, *The President as Interpreter-in-Chief*, 35.

24. See Robert J. Donovan, *Conflict and Crisis: The Presidency of Harry S. Truman, 1945–48* and *Tumultuous Years: The Presidency of Harry S. Truman, 1949–1953*; Michael Lacey, ed., *The Truman Presidency*; Donald R. McCoy, *The Presidency of Harry S. Truman*; and David McCullough, *Truman*.

25. Robert H. Ferrell, ed., *Off the Record: The Private Papers of Harry S. Truman*, 310.

26. John W. Gardner, *On Leadership*, 43.

27. Corwin, *President*, 29–30.

28. Rossiter, *Constitutional Dictatorship* and *The American Presidency*, 15–16; Rossiter, *The American Presidency*, 73.

29. Richard E. Neustadt, *Presidential Power*, 37, 32.

30. See Vaughn Davis Bornet, *The Presidency of Lyndon B. Johnson*; and Eric F. Goodman, *The Tragedy of Lyndon Johnson*.

31. Randall B. Woods, *LBJ: Architect of American Ambition*, 440.

32. See Stephen E. Ambrose, *Nixon*; Michael A. Genovese, *The Nixon Presidency: Power and Politics in the Turbulent Times*; Stanley Kutler, *The Wars of Watergate*; Richard M. Nixon, *RN: The Memoirs of Richard Nixon*; and Michael A. Genovese, *The Watergate Crisis*.

33. Henry Kissinger, *White House Years*, 57. For a more elaborate discussion of presidential policies dealing with relative decline, see Michael A. Genovese, *The Presidency in an Age of Limits*.

34. Robert Osgood et al., *Retreat from Empire?*

35. While Nixon has denied that his policies were designed to face an era of relative decline, he certainly acted as if that were precisely what he and Kissinger were aiming at. Now Nixon has especially harsh words for the

politicians and academics who speak and write about decline. See Richard Nixon, *Victory Without War*.

36. William W. Lammers and Michael A. Genovese, *The Presidency and Domestic Policy: Comparing Leadership Styles, FDR to Clinton*.

37. See Michael A. Genovese and Iwan Morgan, eds., *Watergate Remembered: The Legacy for American Politics*.

38. Arthur M. Schlesinger Jr., *The Imperial Presidency*.

39. See Lou Cannon, *President Reagan: The Role of a Lifetime*; Ronald Reagan, *An American Life*; and Edmund Morris, *Dutch: A Memoir of Ronald Reagan*.

40. Sidney M. Milkis, "Franklin D. Roosevelt, Progressives, and the Limits of Popular Leadership," 14.

41. Jane Mayer and Doyle McManus, *Landslide: The Unmaking of the President, 1984–1986*.

42. Terry Eastland, *Energy in the Executive: The Case for the Strong President*.

Chapter 5

1. The dangerous-branch reference comes from Alexander Hamilton in Federalist No. 78, where he referred to the judiciary as the "least dangerous branch" of government.

2. For a critique, see Robert J. Spitzer, "The Unitary Executive and the Commander-in-Chief."

3. See John C. Yoo's attack against President Clinton's use of presidential power in "The Imperial President Abroad."

4. Traditionally, conservatives have been suspicious of governmental and executive power, but in the 1980s, many conservatives, seeing an opportunity for a strong presidency to be put to conservative use, abandoned principle and called for the enlargement of presidential authority (at least when in the hands of Ronald Reagan). See Eastland, *Energy in the Executive*.

5. See Steven G. Calabresi, Christopher S. Yoo, and Anthony J. Colangelo, "The Unitary Executive in the Modern Era, 1945–2004"; Steven G. Calabresi, Laurence D. Nee, and Christopher S. Yoo, "The Unitary Executive During the Third Half-Century, 1889–1945"; Steven G. Calabresi and Christopher S. Yoo, "The Unitary Executive During the Second Half-Century"; Steven G. Calabresi and Christopher S. Yoo, "The Unitary Executive During the First Half-Century"; and Steven G. Calabresi and Saikrishna B. Prakash, "The President's Power to Execute Laws."

6. See Spitzer, *Saving the Constitution from Lawyers*.

7. *Hirabayashi v. U.S.*, 320 US 81 (1943); *United States v. Robel*, 389 US 258 (1967); *Hamdi v. Rumsfeld*, 542 US 507 (2004).

8. Michael Stokes Paulsen, "The Constitution of Necessity." See also Steven G. Calabresi and Kevin H. Rhodes, "The Structural Constitution: Unitary Executive, Plural Judiciary."

9. Louis Fisher, "Unitary Executive: Ideology Versus the Constitution."

10. See Alan Wolfe, *Does American Democracy Still Work?* 1–12; Sanford Levinson, *Our Undemocratic Constitution*, 49–62, 81–97; Ronald Dworkin, *Is Democracy Possible Here?*; Sheldon Wolin, *Democracy Incorporated: Managed Democracy and the Specter of Inverted Totalitarianism*, 100; and Jeffrey K. Talis and Stephen Macedo, eds., *The Limits of Constitutional Democracy*.

11. See Chris J. Dolan and Betty Glad, eds., *Striking First*.

12. The source of the president's justifications for the exercise of the extraordinary powers can be seen in a series of memos, most of which were written by members of the Office of Legal Counsel. See John C. Yoo, "The President's Constitutional Authority to Conduct Military Operations Against Terrorists and Nations Supporting Them: Memorandum Opinion for the Deputy Counsel of the President"; and Bybee, "Memorandum for Alberto R. Gonzales." On December 30, 2004, the Justice Department issued a new memorandum that repudiated the administration's August 2002 memorandum rejecting the earlier, narrow, view of torture. See "Working Group Report."

13. See Calabresi and Rhodes, "Structural Constitution"; and Steven G. Calabresi and Christopher S. Yoo, *A History of the Unitary Executive: Executive Branch Practice from 1789 to 2004*.

14. A more elaborate description of this can be found in Fisher, "Unitary Executive." I have also attempted to discuss the unitary executive and give a fuller review of its parts in Michael A. Genovese, "Foundations of the Unitary Executive of George W. Bush."

15. See Daniel P. Franklin, *Extraordinary Measures: The Exercise of Prerogative Powers in the United States*.

16. See Michael A. Genovese, "Presidential Leadership and Crisis Management" and "Presidents and Crisis: Developing a Crisis Management System in the Executive Branch."

17. John Locke, *Second Treatise of Civil Government*.

18. See Genovese, *Power of the American Presidency*.

19. Eastland, *Energy in the Executive*.

20. See John C. Yoo, *The Powers of War and Peace: The Constitution and Foreign Affairs After 9/11* and *War by Other Means*.

21. It is here that the Bush efforts to defy law become so relevant. See, for example, the growing literature on presidential "signing statements." See Charles Savage, "Bush Challenges Hundreds of Laws," *Boston Globe*, April 30, 2006, A1; Savage, "Bush Cites Authority to Bypass FEMA Law," *Boston Globe*, October 6, 2006, A1; and Savage, *Takeover: The Return of the Imperial Presidency and the Subversion of American Democracy*, 230.

22. See Michael A. Genovese, "Must a President Obey the Law?"

23. Jane Mayer, "The Hidden Power," 51.

24. See Michael A. Genovese and Robert J. Spitzer, "Re-examining War Powers."

25. See Niccolò Machiavelli, *The Discourse of Livy*, Chapter 34, on the Roman use of temporary dictatorship in times of crisis.

26. Daniel Farber, *Lincoln's Constitution*.

27. See Richard A. Posner, *Not a Suicide Pact: The Constitution in a Time of National Emergency*.

28. *New York Times*, http://www.nytimes.com/ref/international/24memo-guide.html.

29. Quoted in Derek Jinks and David Sloss, "Is the President Bound by the Geneva Conventions?" See also Michael A. Genovese and Iwan Morgan, eds., "Introduction: Remembering Watergate," 1.

30. See, for example, *Rasul v. Bush* 542 US 466 (2004).

31. See Bybee, "Memorandum for Alberto R. Gonzales"; "Standards of Conduct for Interrogation Under 18 US SS 2340–234A"; "Working Group Report"; and "The Memo."

32. See Savage, *Takeover*.

33. Glendon A. Schubert, *The Presidency and the Courts*; Genovese, *Supreme Court*; Louis Fisher, "Judicial Review of the War Power."

34. David Gray Adler, *United States v. Curtiss-Wright*.

35. Rossiter, *Constitutional Dictatorship*.

36. See Michael A. Genovese, "Prerogative in Action: The Lessons of History."

37. "President Speaks," *New York Times*, September 8, 1942.

38. Genovese, *Nixon Presidency*.

39. Center for Public Integrity, "False Pretenses."

40. See 2003 Defense Department memo, often referred to as the "Torture Memo": Memorandum for William J. Haynes IT, General Counsel of the Department of Defense, "Re: Military Interrogation of Alien Unlawful Combatants Held Outside the United States." For this and other memos from the Office of Legal Council, see Karen J. Greenberg and Joshua L. Dratel, *The Torture Papers: The Road to Abu Ghraib*.

41. Yoo, *Powers of War and Peace*, 27; Yoo, *War by Other Means*, xii (emphasis added).

42. For a critique of Yoo's view, see David Luban, "The Defense of Torture," *New York Review of Books*, March 15, 2007, 37–40.

43. The Obama administration has continued with a number of Bush's policies yet has toned down the rhetoric a bit. His antiterrorist polices might be characterized as "Bush lite."

44. See Table 5.1 for the different interpretations of presidential power.

45. Posner and Vermeule, *Executive Unbound*, 5.

46. Ibid., 5, 11, 12, 14, 17, 16.

47. Koh, *National Security Constitution*.

48. Ibid., 69.

49. This book represents such a position, as do Cronin and Genovese, *Paradoxes of the American Presidency*; and Genovese, *Presidential Prerogative*.

50. Andrew Rudalevige, *The New Imperial Presidency: Renewing Presidential Power After Watergate*.

Chapter 6

1. For an examination of the various approaches one might take in reforming the presidency, see Michael A. Genovese, ed., *Contending Approaches to the American Presidency*.

2. Rossiter, *The American Presidency*, 257; Schlesinger, *The Imperial Presidency*, x.

3. *The Federalist Papers*, Nos. 47 and 51.

4. Many of these questions were suggested in Bert A. Rockman, "Reforming the Presidency: Nonproblems and Problems."

5. See Genovese, *Contending Approaches to the American Presidency*.

6. See, for example, James L. Sundquist, *Constitutional Reform*.

7. Rockman, "Reforming the Presidency," 647.

8. Gene Healy, *The Cult of the Presidency: America's Dangerous Devotion to Executive Power*; Koh, *National Security Constitution*, 209.

9. Ryan Barilleaux, "Conservatives and the Presidency."

10. See Yoo, *Powers of War and Peace*; and Posner and Vermeule, *Executive Unbound*.

11. Jules Lobel, "Emergency Power and the Decline of Liberalism"; Robert Spitzer, "Liberalism and the Presidency."

12. See Matthew Crenson and Benjamin Ginsberg, *Presidential Power: Unchecked and Unbalanced*, 354; and Frederick A. O. Schwarz Jr. and Aziz

Z. Huq, *Unchecked and Unbalanced: Presidential Power in a Time of Terror*, 203–206.

13. Bruce Ackerman, *Before the Next Attack*.

14. Jack Valenti, "A Six-Year Presidency?"

15. Woodrow Wilson, letter placed in the *Congressional Record*, 64th Cong., 2nd sess., August 15, 1916.

16. James MacGregor Burns, "Keeping the President in Line," *New York Times*, April 8, 1973, E15.

17. See Jonah Leher, *How We Decide*.

18. Koh, *National Security Constitution*, 167.

19. Rudalevige, *New Imperial Presidency*, 275.

20. Ackerman, *Before the Next Attack*, 105; Koh, *National Security Constitution*, 181–182.

21. *N.Y. Times Co. v. United States*, 403 US 713 (1971).

Chapter 7

1. Genovese, *Presidential Prerogative*.

2. Posner and Vermeule, *Executive Unbound*.

3. Schlesinger, *War and the American Presidency*, 66.

4. Michael Lind, "The Out-of-Control Presidency."

5. Benjamin R. Barber, "Neither Leaders nor Followers," 117.

Appendix 2

1. An earlier and slightly different version of this model appeared in Michael A. Genovese, "Presidential Leadership: A Dyadic Model."

BIBLIOGRAPHY

Ackerman, Bruce. *Before the Next Attack*. New Haven, CT: Yale University Press, 2006.

Adler, David Gray. "The Constitutional Presidency." In *Contending Approaches to the American Presidency*, edited by Michael A. Genovese. Washington, DC: CQ Press, 2012.

———. *United States v. Curtiss-Wright*. Lawrence: University Press of Kansas, forthcoming.

Ambrose, Stephen E. *Nixon*. 3 vols. New York: Simon & Schuster, 1989, 1991, 1995.

Bailey, Jeremy David. "Executive Prerogative and the 'Good Officer' in Thomas Jefferson's Letter to John B. Colvin." *Presidential Studies Quarterly* 24, no. 4 (2004).

Bailyn, Bernard. *The Ideological Origins of the American Revolution*. Cambridge, MA: Harvard University Press, 1967.

Baker, Ray Stannard. *Woodrow Wilson*. London: Heineman, 1932.

Balleck, Barry J. "When the Ends Justify the Means: Thomas Jefferson and the Louisiana Purchase." *Presidential Studies Quarterly* 22, no. 4 (1992): 679–696.

Barber, Benjamin R. "Neither Leaders nor Followers." In *Essays in Honor of James MacGregor Burns*, edited by Thomas E. Cronin and Michael R. Beschloss. Englewood Cliffs, NJ: Prentice-Hall, 1989.

Barilleaux, Ryan. "Conservatives and the Presidency." In *Contending Approaches to the Presidency*, edited by Michael A. Genovese. Washington, DC: CQ Press, 2012.

Beard, Charles, and Mary Beard. *The Rise of American Civilization*. New York: Macmillan, 1933.

Bergeron, Paul H. *The Presidency of James K. Polk*. Lawrence: University Press of Kansas, 1987.

Bessette, Joseph M., and Jeffrey Tulis. *The Presidency in the Constitutional Order*. Baton Rouge: Louisiana State University Press, 1981.

Bornet, Vaughn Davis. *The Presidency of Lyndon B. Johnson*. Lawrence: University Press of Kansas, 1983.

Brands, H. W. *T. R.: The Last Romantic*. New York: Basic Books, 1997.

Brookhiser, Richard. *Founding Father: Rediscovering George Washington*. New York: Free Press, 1996.

Bruce, Robert V. *Lincoln and the Tools of War*. Indianapolis: Bobbs-Merrill, 1956.

Bryce, James. *The American Commonwealth*. New York: Macmillan, 1888.

Bybee, Jay S., Assistant Attorney General, US Department of Justice. "Memorandum for Alberto R. Gonzales." August 1, 2002. http://www.washington post.com/wp-srv/nation/documents/dojinterrogationmemo20020801.pdf.

Calabresi, Steven G., Laurence D. Nee, and Christopher S. Yoo. "The Unitary Executive During the Third Half-Century, 1889–1945." *Notre Dame Law Review* 80 (2004).

Calabresi, Steven G., and Saikrishna B. Prakash. "The President's Power to Execute Laws." *Yale Law Journal* 104 (1994).

Calabresi, Steven G., and Kevin H. Rhodes. "The Structural Constitution: Unitary Executive, Plural Judiciary." *Harvard Law Review* 105 (1992).

Calabresi, Steven G., and Christopher S. Yoo. *A History of the Unitary Executive: Executive Branch Practice from 1789 to 2004*. New Haven, CT: Yale University Press, 2008.

———. "The Unitary Executive During the First Half-Century." *Case Western Reserve Law Review* 47 (1997).

———. "The Unitary Executive During the Second Half-Century." *Harvard Journal of Law and Public Policy* 26 (2003).

Calabresi, Steven G., Christopher S. Yoo, and Anthony J. Colangelo. "The Unitary Executive in the Modern Era, 1945–2004." *Iowa Law Review* 90 (2004).

Cannon, Lou. *President Reagan: The Role of a Lifetime*. New York: Simon & Schuster, 1989.

Cappon, Lester J. *The Adams-Jefferson Letters: The Complete Correspondence Between Thomas Jefferson and Abigail and John Adams*. Chapel Hill: University of North Carolina Press, 1959.

Center for Public Integrity. "False Pretenses." https://www.publicintegrity .org/warcard/.

Chambers, William N. "Jackson." In *America's Ten Greatest Presidents*, edited by Morton Borden. Chicago: Rand McNally, 1961.

Clements, Kendrick A. *The Presidency of Woodrow Wilson*. Lawrence: University Press of Kansas, 1992.

Corwin, Edward S. *The President: Office and Powers, 1787–1984*. New York: New York University Press, 1940.

———. *Total War and the Constitution*. New York: Alfred A. Knopf, 1947.

Crenson, Matthew, and Benjamin Ginsberg. *Presidential Power: Unchecked and Unbalanced*. New York: W. W. Norton, 2007.

Cronin, Thomas E., ed. *Inventing the American Presidency*. Lawrence: University Press of Kansas, 1989.

———. *The State of the Presidency*. Boston: Little, Brown, 1980.

Cronin, Thomas E., and Michael A. Genovese. *The Paradoxes of the American Presidency*. 4th ed. New York: Oxford University Press, 2012.

Cunningham, Noble E., Jr. *In Pursuit of Reason: The Life of Thomas Jefferson*. New York: Ballantine, 1987.

Dolan, Chris J., and Betty Glad, eds. *Striking First*. New York: Palgrave Macmillan, 2005.

Dolce, Philip C., and George H. Skau, eds. *Power and the Presidency*. New York: Scribner's Sons, 1976.

Donald, David Herbert. *Lincoln*. New York: Touchstone, 1995.

Donovan, Robert J. *Conflict and Crisis: The Presidency of Harry S. Truman, 1945–48*. New York: W. W. Norton, 1977.

———. *Tumultuous Years: The Presidency of Harry S. Truman, 1949–1953*. New York: W. W. Norton, 1982.

Dworkin, Ronald. *Is Democracy Possible Here?* Princeton, NJ: Princeton University Press, 2006.

Eastland, Terry. *Energy in the Executive: The Case for the Strong President*. New York: Free Press, 1992.

Evans, Harold. *The American Century*. New York: Alfred A. Knopf, 1998.

Farber, Daniel. *Lincoln's Constitution*. Chicago: University Press of Chicago, 2003.

Ferrell, Robert H., ed. *Off the Record: The Private Papers of Harry S. Truman*. Columbia: University of Missouri Press, 1997.

Fisher, Louis. *The Constitution Between Friends*. New York: St. Martin's Press, 1978.

———. "Judicial Review of the War Power." *Presidential Studies Quarterly* 35 (September 2005): 466–495.

———. "The Unitary Executive: Ideology Versus the Constitution." In *The Unitary Executive and the Modern Presidency*, edited by Ryan J. Barilleaux and Christopher S. Kelley, 17–40. College Station: Texas A&M University Press, 2010.

Flexner, James Thomas. *Washington: The Indispensible Man*. Boston: Little, Brown, 1974.

Franklin, Daniel P. *Extraordinary Measures: The Exercise of Prerogative Powers in the United States*. Pittsburgh: University of Pittsburgh Press, 1991.

Gardner, John W. *On Leadership*. New York: Simon and Schuster, 1990.

Genovese, Michael A., ed. *Contending Approaches to the American Presidency*. Washington, DC: CQ Press, 2012.

———. "Foundations of the Unitary Executive of George W. Bush." In *The Unitary Executive and the Modern Presidency*, edited by Ryan J. Barilleaux and Christopher S. Kelley, 125–144. College Station: Texas A&M University Press, 2010.

———. "Must a President Obey the Law?" *White House Studies* 8, no. 1 (2008): 3–17.

———. *The Nixon Presidency: Power and Politics in Turbulent Times*. Westport, CT: Greenwood Press, 1990.

———. *The Power of the American Presidency, 1789–2000*. New York: Oxford University Press, 2000.

———. "Prerogative in Action: The Lessons of History." In *Presidential Prerogative: Imperial Power in an Age of Terrorism*, 92–126. Stanford, CA: Stanford University Press, 2011.

———. *The Presidency in an Age of Limits*. Westport, CT: Greenwood Press, 1993.

———. "Presidential Leadership: A Dyadic Model." In *Leadership at the Crossroads: Leadership and Politics*, edited by Michael A. Genovese and Lori C. Han, 77–98. Westport, CT: Praeger, 2008.

———. "Presidential Leadership and Crisis Management." *Presidential Studies Quarterly* 16, no. 2 (1986): 300–309.

———. *Presidential Prerogative: Imperial Power in an Age of Terrorism*. Stanford, CA: Stanford University Press, 2011.

———. "Presidents and Crisis: Developing a Crisis Management System in the Executive Branch." *International Journal on World Peace* (Spring 1987): 108–117.

———. *The Supreme Court, the Constitution, and Presidential Power*. Lanham, MD: University Press of America, 1980.

———. *The Watergate Crisis*. Westport, CT: Greenwood Press, 1999.

———, ed. "William McKinley." In *The Encyclopedia of the American Presidency*. New York: Facts-on-File, 2004.

Genovese, Michael A., and Iwan Morgan, eds. "Introduction: Remembering Watergate." In *Watergate Remembered: The Legacy for American Politics*. New York: Palgrave Macmillan, 2011.

———. *Watergate Remembered: The Legacy for American Politics*. New York: Palgrave Macmillan, 2012.

Genovese, Michael A., and Robert J. Spitzer. "Re-examining War Powers." *PRG Newsletter* 30, no. 1 (2006).

Goodman, Eric F. *The Tragedy of Lyndon Johnson*. New York: Dell, 1968.

Gould, Lewis L. *The Presidency of Theodore Roosevelt*. Lawrence: University Press of Kansas, 1991.

Greenberg, Karen J., and Joshua L. Dratel. *The Torture Papers: The Road to Abu Ghraib*. New York: Cambridge University Press, 2005.

Hay, John. *Lincoln and the Civil War*. New York: Dodd, Mead, 1939.

Healy, Gene. *The Cult of the Presidency: America's Dangerous Devotion to Executive Power*. Washington, DC: Cato Institute, 2008.

Heckscher, August. *Woodrow Wilson*. New York: Collier, 1991.

Jefferson, Thomas. *Notes on the State of Virginia*. New York: Harper & Row, 1964.

Jinks, Derek, and David Sloss. "Is the President Bound by the Geneva Conventions?" *Cornell Law Reviews* 90 (2004).

Ketcham, Ralph. *Presidents Above Party*. Chapel Hill: University of North Carolina Press, 1984.

Kissinger, Henry. *White House Years*. Boston: Little, Brown, 1979.

Koh, Harold Hongju. *The National Security Constitution: Sharing Power After the Iran-Contra Affair*. New Haven, CT: Yale University Press, 1990.

Kutler, Stanley. *The Wars of Watergate*. New York: Alfred A. Knopf, 1990.

Lacey, Michael, ed. *The Truman Presidency*. New York: Cambridge University Press, 1989.

Lammers, William W., and Michael A. Genovese. Washington, DC: Congressional Quarterly, 2000.

Lamon, Ward H. *Recollections of Abraham Lincoln*. New York: Century, 1911.

Latner, Richard. *The Presidency of Andrew Jackson: White House Politics, 1829–1837*. Athens: University of Georgia Press, 1979.

Leher, Jonah. *How We Decide*. New York: Houghton, Mifflin, Harcourt, 2010.

Levinson, Sanford. *Our Undemocratic Constitution*. New York: Oxford University Press, 2006.

Liell, Scott. *46 Pages: Thomas Paine, Common Sense, and the Turning Point to Independence*. Philadelphia: Running Press, 2003.

Lincoln, Abraham. *Abraham Lincoln: Speeches and Writings, 1859–1865*. New York: Library of America, 1989.

———. "Special Session Message, July 4, 1861." In *Borzoi Reader in American Politics*, edited by Edward Keynes and David Adamany. New York: Alfred A. Knopf, 1973.

————. "Special Session Message, July 4, 1861." In *A Compilation of the Messages and Papers of the Presidents*, edited by James D. Richardson, 7:3227–3232. New York: Bureau of National Literature, 1897.

Lind, Michael. "The Out-of-Control Presidency." *New Republic*, August 14, 1995, 18–23.

Lobel, Jules. "Emergency Power and the Decline of Liberalism." *Yale Law Journal* 98 (1989): 1426–1427.

Locke, John. *Second Treatise of Civil Government*. Edited by Peter Laslett. Cambridge: Cambridge University Press, 1960.

Lockwood, Henry Clay. *The Abolition of the Presidency*. New York: R. Worthington, 1884.

Machiavelli, Niccolò. *The Discourse of Livy*. Translated by Harvey C. Mansfield and Nathan Tarcov. Chicago: University Press of Chicago, 1995.

Marlowe, Melanie. "The Unitary Executive." In *Contending Approaches to the American Presidency*, edited by Michael A. Genovese. Washington, DC: CQ Press, 2012.

Matheson, Scott M., Jr. *Presidential Constitutionalism in Perilous Times*. Cambridge, MA: Harvard University Press, 2009.

Mayer, David N. "Jefferson and Separation of Powers." In *The Presidency Then and Now*, edited by Philip G. Henderson. Lanham, MD: Rowman and Littlefield, 2000.

Mayer, Jane. "The Hidden Power." *New Yorker*, July 3, 2006.

Mayer, Jane, and Doyle McManus. *Landslide: The Unmaking of the President, 1984–1986*. Boston: Houghton Mifflin, 1988.

McCormac, Eugene I. *James K. Polk: A Political Biography*. Berkeley and Los Angeles: University of California Press, 1922.

McCoy, Charles A. *Polk and the Presidency*. Austin: University of Texas Press, 1960.

McCoy, Donald R. *The Presidency of Harry S. Truman*. Lawrence: University Press of Kansas, 1984.

McCullough, David. *Truman*. New York: Harper & Row, 1987.

McPherson, James M. *Abraham Lincoln and the Second American Revolution*. New York: Oxford University Press, 1991.

Means, Cyril C., Jr. "Is Presidency Barred to Americans Born Abroad?" *U.S. News & World Report*, December 23, 1955, 26–30.

"The Memo." *New Yorker*, February 27, 2006.

Milkis, Sidney M. "Franklin D. Roosevelt, Progressives, and the Limits of Popular Leadership." In *Speaking to the People: The Rhetorical Presidency in His-*

torical Perspective, edited by Richard J. Ellis. Amherst: University of Massachusetts Press, 1988.

Milkis, Sidney M., and Michael Nelson. *The American Presidency*. Washington, DC: Congressional Quarterly, 1994.

Millard, Candice. *The River of Doubt: Theodore Roosevelt's Darkest Journey*. New York: Anchor, 2005.

Miller, Matthew. *Theodore Roosevelt: A Life*. New York: Quill, 1992.

Miroff, Bruce. *Icons of Democracy*. New York: Basic Books, 1993.

Morris, Edmund. *Dutch: A Memoir of Ronald Reagan*. New York: Random House, 1999.

Neely, Mark. *The Fate of Liberty*. New York: Oxford University Press, 1991.

Neustadt, Richard E. *Presidential Power*. New York: Wiley, 1960.

Nixon, Richard M. *RN: The Memoirs of Richard Nixon*. New York: Grosset and Dunlop, 1978.

———. *Victory Without War*. New York: Simon & Schuster, 1998.

Osgood, Robert, et al. *Retreat from Empire?* Baltimore, MD: Johns Hopkins University Press, 1973.

Paludan, Phillip Shaw. *The Presidency of Abraham Lincoln*. Lawrence: University Press of Kansas, 1994.

Paulsen, Michael Stokes. "The Constitution of Necessity." *Notre Dame Law Review* 79 (July 2004).

Peterson, Merrill D. *Thomas Jefferson and the New Nation*. New York: Oxford University Press, 1970.

Posner, Eric A., and Adrian Vermeule. *The Executive Unbound: After the Madisonian Republic*. New York: Oxford University Press, 2010.

Posner, Richard A. *Not a Suicide Pact: The Constitution in a Time of National Emergency*. New York: Oxford University Press, 2006.

Randall, J. G., and Richard N. Current. *Lincoln: The President*. 2 vols. New York: Da Capo, 1997.

Reagan, Ronald. *An American Life*. New York: Simon & Schuster, 1990.

Remini, Robert V. *Andrew Jackson and the Course of American Democracy, 1833–1845*. New York: Harper & Row, 1984.

———. *Andrew Jackson and the Course of American Empire, 1767–1821*. New York: Harper & Row, 1984.

———. *Andrew Jackson and the Course of American Freedom, 1822–1832*. New York: Harper & Row, 1984.

———. "Election of 1832." In *History of American Presidential Elections, 1789–1968*, edited by Arthur M. Schlesinger Jr. New York: Chelsea House, 1971.

Risjord, Norman K. *Thomas Jefferson*. Madison, WI: Madison House, 1994.

Robinson, Donald L. *"To the Best of My Ability": The Presidency and the Constitution*. New York: W. W. Norton, 1987.

Rockman, Bert A. *The Leadership Question: The Presidency and the American System*. New York: Praeger, 1985.

———. "Reforming the Presidency: Nonproblems and Problems." *PS* 20, no. 3 (1987): 643–649.

Roosevelt, Theodore. *An Autobiography*. New York: Charles Scribner's Sons, 1925.

———. *The Works of Theodore Roosevelt*. New York: Scribner's, 1926.

Rose, Gary L. *The American Presidency Under Siege*. Albany: State University of New York Press, 1997.

Rossiter, Clinton. *The American Presidency*. New York: Harcourt, Brace, & World, 1956.

———. *Constitutional Dictatorship: Crisis Government in the Modern Democracies*. Princeton, NJ: Princeton University Press, 1948.

———. *The Supreme Court and the Commander in Chief*. Ithaca, NY: Cornell University Press, 1976.

Rudalevige, Andrew. *The New Imperial Presidency: Renewing Presidential Power After Watergate*. Ann Arbor: University of Michigan Press, 2005.

Savage, Charles. *Takeover: The Return of the Imperial Presidency and the Subversion of American Democracy*. New York: Little, Brown, 2007.

Schlesinger, Arthur M., Jr. *The Age of Jackson*. Boston: Little, Brown, 1946.

———. *The Imperial Presidency*. Boston: Houghton Mifflin, 1973.

———. *War and the American Presidency*. New York: W. W. Norton, 2004.

Schubert, Glendon A. *The Presidency and the Courts*. Minneapolis: University of Minnesota Press, 1957.

Schwarz, Frederick A. O., Jr., and Aziz Z. Huq. *Unchecked and Unbalanced: Presidential Power in a Time of Terror*. New York: New Press, 2007.

Sellers, Charles G. *James K. Polk: Continentalist, 1843–1846*. Princeton, NJ: Princeton University Press, 1966.

Smith, Richard Norton. *Patriarch: George Washington and the New Nation*. Boston: Houghton Mifflin, 1933.

Spalding, Matthew. *The Founder's Almanac*. Washington, DC: Heritage Foundation, 2002.

Spitzer, Robert J. "Liberalism and the Presidency." In *Contending Approaches to the American Presidency*, edited by Michael A. Genovese. Washington, DC: CQ Press, 2012.

———. *The Presidential Veto: Touchstone of the American Presidency*. Albany: State University of New York Press, 1988.

———. *Saving the Constitution from Lawyers*, 90–128. Cambridge: Cambridge University Press, 2008.

———. "The Unitary Executive and the Commander-in-Chief." In *Saving the Constitution from Lawyers*, 90–128. Cambridge: Cambridge University Press, 2008.

"Standards of Conduct for Interrogation Under 18 U.S.C. SS 2340–2340A." August 1, 2002. http://www.justice.gov/olc/18USC23402340a2.htm.

Stuckey, Mary. *The President as Interpreter-in-Chief*. Chaltham, NJ: Chaltham House, 1991.

Sundquist, James L. *Constitutional Reform*. Washington, DC: Brookings Institution, 1986.

Taft, William Howard. *The President and His Powers*. New York: Columbia University Press, 1916.

Talis, Jeffrey K., and Stephen Macedo, eds. *The Limits of Constitutional Democracy*. Princeton, NJ: Princeton University Press, 2010.

Thach, Charles C. *The Creation of the Presidency, 1775–1789: A Study in Constitutional History*. Baltimore, MD: Johns Hopkins University Press, 1922.

Tocqueville, Alexis de. *Democracy in America*. Garden City, NJ: Doubleday, 1969.

Tourtellot, Arthur Bernon. *The Presidents on the Presidency*. New York: Russell & Russell, 1970.

Tuchman, Barbara W. "The British Lose America." Chapter 4 of *The March of Folly*. New York: Ballantine, 1984.

Valenti, Jack. "A Six-Year Presidency?" *Newsweek*, February 4, 1971, 11.

Walworth, Arthur. *Woodrow Wilson*. New York: W. W. Norton, 1978.

White, Leonard. *The Jacksonians: A Study in Administrative History, 1829–1861*. New York: Macmillan, 1954.

Whitman, Wilson, arr. *Jefferson's Letters*. Eau Claire, WI: Hale, 1940.

Wills, Garry. *Lincoln at Gettysburg: The Words That Remade America*. New York: Simon & Schuster, 1992.

Wilson, Woodrow. *Congressional Government: A Study in American Politics*. New York: Meridian Books, 1885.

———. *Constitutional Government in the United States*. New York: Columbia University Press, 1908.

Wolfe, Alan. *Does American Democracy Still Work?* New Haven, CT: Yale University Press, 2006.

———. "Presidential Power and the Crisis of Modernization." *Democracy* 1, no. 2 (1981).

Wolin, Sheldon. *Democracy Incorporated: Managed Democracy and the Specter of Inverted Totalitarianism*. Princeton, NJ: Princeton University Press, 2008.

Woods, Randall B. *LBJ: Architect of American Ambition*. New York Free Press, 2006.

"Working Group Report on Detainee Interrogations in the Global War on Terrorism: Assessment of Legal, Historical, Policy, and Operational Considerations." April 4, 2003. http://www.defenselink.mil/news/Jun2004622 doc8.pdf.

Yoo, John C. "The Imperial President Abroad." In *The Rule of Law in the Wake of Clinton*, edited by Roger Pilon. Washington, DC: Cato Institute, 2000.

———. *The Powers of War and Peace: The Constitution and Foreign Affairs After 9/11*. Chicago: University of Chicago Press, 2005.

———. "The President's Constitutional Authority to Conduct Military Operations Against Terrorists and Nations Supporting Them: Memorandum Opinion for the Deputy Counsel of the President." September 25, 2001. http://www.usdoj.olc/warpowers925.htm.

———. *War by Other Means*. New York: Atlantic Monthly Press, 2006.

INDEX